The Origami Garden

The Origami Garden

Amazing Flowers, Leaves, Bugs, and Other Backyard Critters

Ioana Stoian

ST. MARTIN'S GRIFFIN
NEW YORK

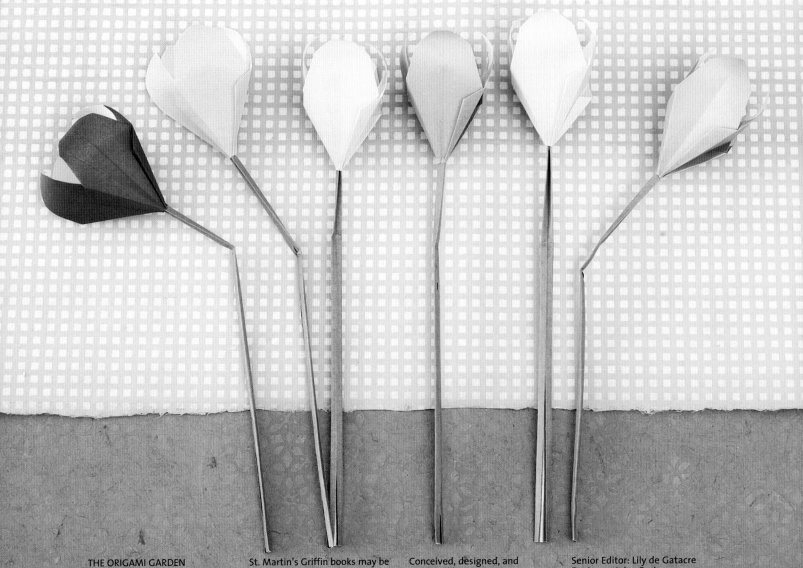

THE ORIGAMI GARDEN

A Quarto Book
Copyright © 2016 Quarto Inc.
All rights reserved.

Printed in China. For information,
address St. Martin's Press,
175 Fifth Avenue, New York,
N.Y. 10010.

www.stmartins.com

Library of Congress Cataloging-in-
Publication Data Available Upon
Request

ISBN: 978-1-250-06877-4

St. Martin's Griffin books may be
purchased for educational,
business, or promotional use. For
information on bulk purchases,
please contact Macmillan
Corporate and Premium Sales
Department at 1-800-221-7945,
extension 5442, or write
specialmarkets@macmillan.com.

First U.S. Edition: January 2016

10 9 8 7 6 5 4 3 2 1

Conceived, designed, and
produced by
Quarto Publishing plc
The Old Brewery
6 Blundell Street
London N7 9BH

QUAR.FTOF

Senior Editor: Lily de Gatacre
Designer: John Grain
Copyeditor: Claire Waite Brown
Illustrator: John Woodcock
Photographer: Simon Pask
Proofreader: Liz Jones
Design Assistant: Martina Calvio
Indexer: Helen Snaith

Art Director: Caroline Guest
Creative Director: Moira Clinch
Publisher: Paul Carslake

Color separation in Hong Kong by
Bright Arts Ltd
Printed in China by Shanghai
Offset Printing Products Ltd

Contents

Meet Ioana

Pick up a piece of paper and fold it in half. Did you hear that noise? It's the sound of that piece of paper changing forever. The crease you have just made cannot be removed nor ironed out. With a few more folds you can create a flower, an animal, a box, a piece of jewelry ... the list is endless. That is what I love about origami: the magical transformation of a piece of paper into something new without adding or removing anything. And yes, I love the sounds that accompany the process!

Eight years ago, I found myself lost in Kyoto, Japan. I stumbled upon a hidden paper studio where an elderly Japanese woman was folding origami cranes; she waved me in and shared her passion with me. I've been folding paper ever since.

Manipulating paper on a daily basis naturally led to a fascination with the material itself. Today, I am a full-time paper artist creating large-scale artworks from my handmade paper. I thoroughly enjoy making a big sheet of paper and then folding it using my entire body; feet pinning down one corner and arms outstretched to deal with the other. I work in a very intuitive manner and most of my origami models are created in the same fashion! Other times the process can be challenging and lengthy, like solving a complicated jigsaw puzzle.

People work in different ways and there are infinite ways to transform a square of paper. In this book, you'll find traditional models, some of my own designs, and contemporary creations by other origami artists. I hope that this carefully chosen selection inspires you and, most of all, I hope that you enjoy folding flowers, birds, and friendly animals to create your own little origami sanctuary.

Ioana

Washing day

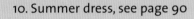

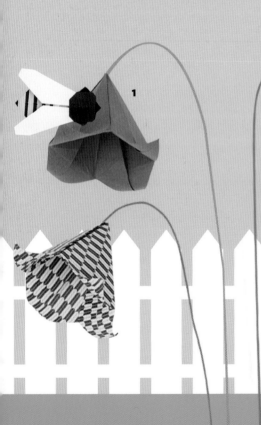

A sunny afternoon

1

2

3

4

By the pond

In the garden

Symbols

Symbols are the language of origami—they will show you exactly what needs to be done and where at each stage. See Steps 1–4 on page 26 to learn how to create the common waterbomb base. Steps 1–4 on page 52 will teach you how to create the square base (also know as the preliminary base).

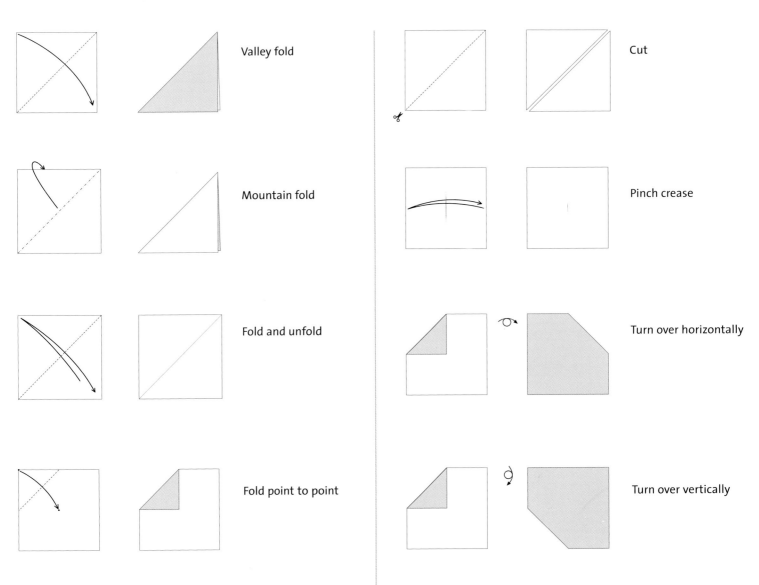

Valley fold

Mountain fold

Fold and unfold

Fold point to point

Cut

Pinch crease

Turn over horizontally

Turn over vertically

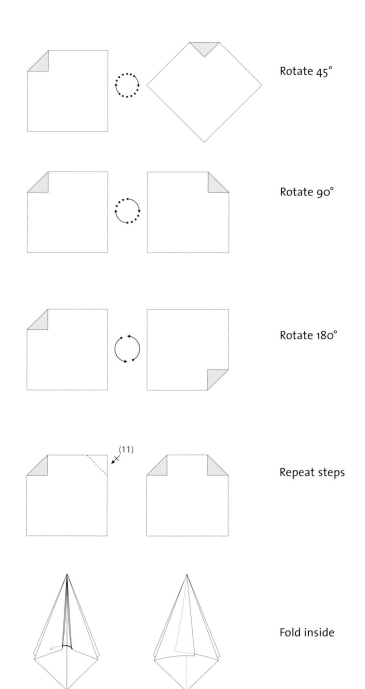

Rotate 45°

Rotate 90°

Rotate 180°

Repeat steps

Fold inside

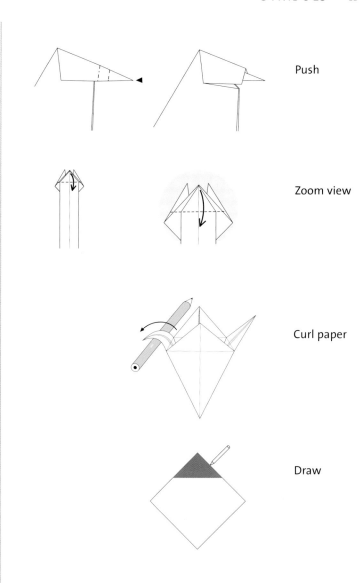

Push

Zoom view

Curl paper

Draw

Meet the projects

There are more than 40 delightful origami projects waiting for you in the pages of this book. Whether you want to create an origami flower garden full of pretty blooms and delicate leaves, or make your own origami menagerie of backyard critters, you'll find the project for you. The following seven pages will give you a quick overview of each finished project, as well as flagging its skill level and page number so you can find the pieces that inspire you, and get folding. Why not turn to the panorama scenes on pages 8–15 to get some inspiration for which projects will work well together to bring your garden scene to life? Flick through, find something that catches your eye, choose your paper, and start folding.

PROJECTS LISTED BY SKILL LEVEL
Are you new to origami, or are you confident in your folding skills and ready for a new challenge? Use this table to choose your projects based on their level of complexity.

Little bird's egg

PAGE 26

SKILL LEVEL 2

Bird's nest

PAGE 28

SKILL LEVEL 1

Fall leaf

PAGE 30

SKILL LEVEL 1

Decorative leaf

PAGE 32

SKILL LEVEL 1

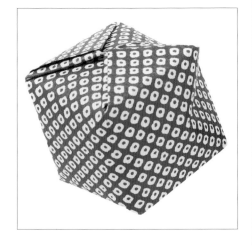

Slow snail

PAGE 33

SKILL LEVEL 2

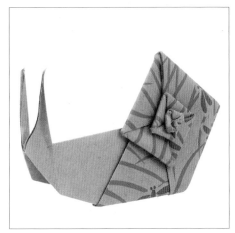

Jumping frog

PAGE 37

SKILL LEVEL 2

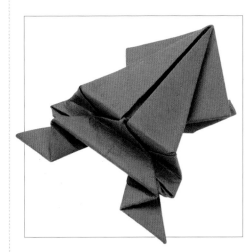

continued ▶

Little ladybug

PAGE 40

SKILL LEVEL 1

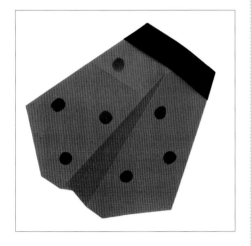

Greedy caterpillar

PAGE 42

SKILL LEVEL 1

Striking butterfly

PAGE 44

SKILL LEVEL 2

Busy bee

PAGE 46

SKILL LEVEL 3

Tasty mushroom

PAGE 50

SKILL LEVEL 2

Early crocus

PAGE 52

SKILL LEVEL 2

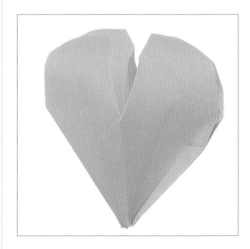

Crocus leaf

PAGE 55

SKILL LEVEL 2

Spring tulip

PAGE 56

SKILL LEVEL 2

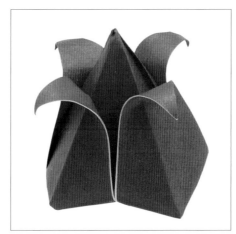

Tulip stem

PAGE 59

SKILL LEVEL 2

Stylized carnation

PAGE 60

SKILL LEVEL 2

Carnation stem

PAGE 62

SKILL LEVEL 2

Pretty flower

PAGE 64

SKILL LEVEL 3

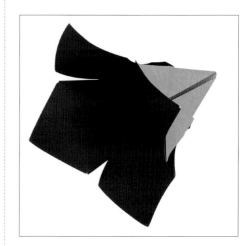

continued ▶

Dainty bellflower

PAGE 66

SKILL LEVEL 3

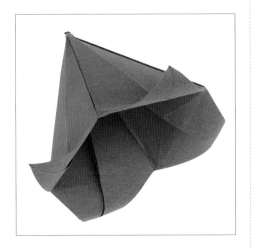

Fragrant lily

PAGE 69

SKILL LEVEL 3

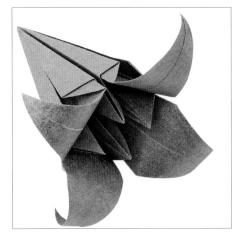

Flower in full bloom

PAGE 72

SKILL LEVEL 2

Proud crow

PAGE 74

SKILL LEVEL 2

Hungry pigeon

PAGE 76

SKILL LEVEL 2

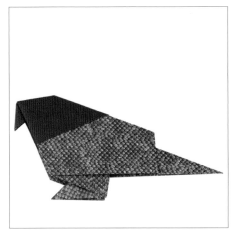

Jenny wren

PAGE 79

SKILL LEVEL 3

Night owls

PAGE 82

SKILL LEVEL 3

Perching branch

PAGE 85

SKILL LEVEL 3

Pair of pants

PAGE 86

SKILL LEVEL 1

Simple underpants

PAGE 87

SKILL LEVEL 1

Short-sleeved shirt

PAGE 88

SKILL LEVEL 1

Smart socks

PAGE 89

SKILL LEVEL 1

continued ▶

Summer dress

PAGE 90

SKILL LEVEL 3

Spinning pinwheel

PAGE 92

SKILL LEVEL 1

Mini watering can

PAGE 94

SKILL LEVEL 3

Miniature trowel

PAGE 98

SKILL LEVEL 2

Flower box

PAGE 107

SKILL LEVEL 3

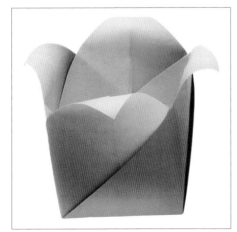

Useful basket

PAGE 104

SKILL LEVEL 3

Practical pot

PAGE 101

SKILL LEVEL 2

Sitting dog

PAGE 110

SKILL LEVEL 1

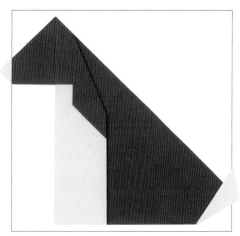

Pet cat

PAGE 112

SKILL LEVEL 3

Friendly bunny

PAGE 116

SKILL LEVEL 3

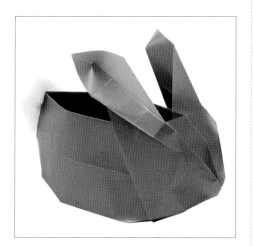

Acrobatic squirrel

PAGE 121

SKILL LEVEL 3

Little bird's egg

This traditional origami model is most commonly referred to as the waterbomb. It is a fun design that can be turned into a hanging decoration, a pendant, or an earring . . . and, of course, a water balloon.

Skill level: 2

Learn how to create the waterbomb base here.

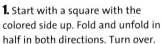

1. Start with a square with the colored side up. Fold and unfold in half in both directions. Turn over.

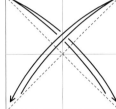

2. Fold and unfold both diagonals.

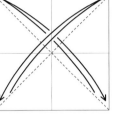

3. Collapse by bringing the top edge down to the bottom edge as you push the sides in.

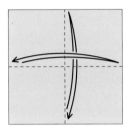

4. This is the waterbomb base. To create a waterbomb base with the white side facing outward, begin Step 1 with the white side up.

5. Fold the left- and right-hand corners of the top layer up to the top of the triangle.

6. Bring the tip of the triangle down to the bottom edge and pinch the center. Unfold.

7. Fold the left- and right-hand points of the diamond to the center pinch mark, but make sure not to go beyond it.

8. Fold the top two small flaps down to the center.

9. Now insert these flaps all the way into the pockets made in Step 7.

Note: To make eggs that will fit nicely into a folded nest, you will need paper squares that are one-quarter of the size of those used for the nest on pages 28–29.

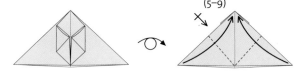

10. Turn over.

11. Repeat Steps 5–9 on this side.

12. When both sides are complete your model will look like this.

13. Hold the model like a propeller using both hands, and blow into the hole.

You could turn your egg into a beautiful bauble by threading a piece of string through the hole.

Bird's nest

This traditional Japanese box makes a cozy nest for little paper eggs (see pages 26–27). You can also fill it with chocolates and other treats for special occasions.

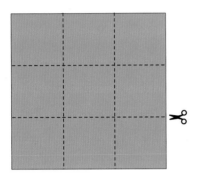

1. Start with a square with the colored side up. Divide the square into a 3:3 grid and cut off the bottom section to create a 2:3 rectangle.

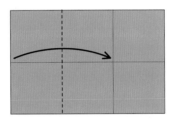

2. With the colored side still facing upward, use the existing folds to bring the left-hand edge over to the second vertical crease line.

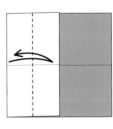

3. Fold this section in half vertically. Unfold.

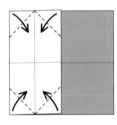

4. Fold all four corners to the crease formed in Step 3.

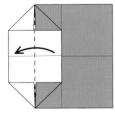

5. Fold the right-hand edge back over to the left along the existing crease. Make sure the corners stay inside.

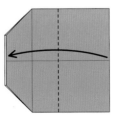

6. Fold the right-hand raw edge to the left-hand raw edge.

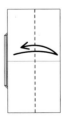

7. Fold this section in half vertically. Unfold.

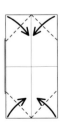

8. Fold all four corners to the crease formed in Step 7.

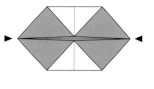

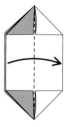
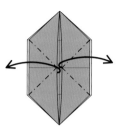

9. Fold the left-hand edge to the right using the existing crease, making sure the corners remain inside.

10. From the center, pull both sides simultaneously to the outside.

11. Flatten, then push the points back toward the center.

This container is very practical for parties. When not in use, collapse it back to Step 10 and store it away until next time.

Reds and yellows give these leaves a realistic, autumnal appearance.
Shades of green would look great for spring and summer leaves.

Fall leaf

Fall is the season when the garden starts to change color and the leaves start to tumble from the trees. This traditional leaf is nice and simple. You'll be making a huge pile before you know it!

Skill level: 1

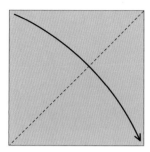

1. Start with a square with the colored side up. Fold in half diagonally.

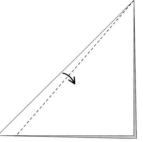

2. Fold the folded edge over starting at the top point and gradually getting slightly wider.

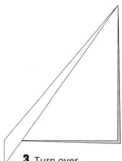

3. Turn over.

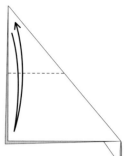

4. Keep both flaps together and fold the top point down to the bottom corner. Unfold.

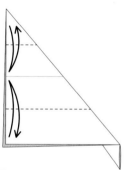

5. Fold the top point and the bottom edges to the central crease made in Step 4. Unfold and turn over.

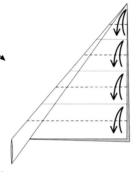

6. Divide each section in half by folding to the existing creases and unfolding. You will end up with a zigzag running from top to bottom.

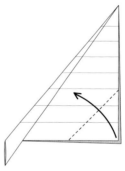

7. Fold the bottom right corner of the top flap up to the third horizontal crease.

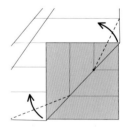

8. Fold the bottom corner of the flap made in Step 7 to the first horizontal crease. Make another fold between the dot and the fourth crease.

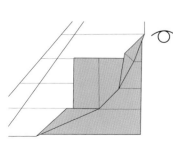

9. Turn over.

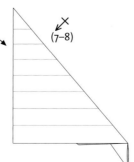

10. Repeat Steps 7–8 on this side.

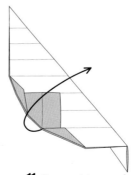

11. Open out to reveal the leaf.

Decorative leaf

There are many kinds of leaves in the garden, in a gorgeous array of colors. This traditional model is a classic and can be folded from any kind of paper. You can make two leaves from one square—perfect for a pair of earrings!

Skill level: 1

1. Start with a square with the colored side up. Fold and unfold in half diagonally, then cut along the crease to obtain two identical triangles. We will only fold one at a time.

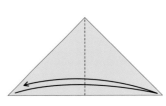

2. With the colored side up, fold and unfold in half vertically.

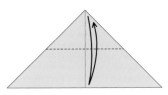

3. Fold the top point down to the center of the bottom edge. Unfold.

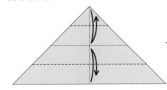

4. Fold the top point and the bottom edge to meet the horizontal crease. Unfold and turn over.

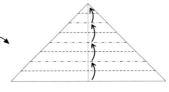

5. Fold the bottom edge up to meet the first mountain crease. Continue to divide the remaining three sections in half, with the final fold meeting the top point, creating a zigzag effect that folds all the layers together.

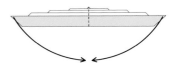

6. Fold the long section in half along the existing central crease.

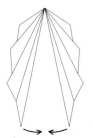

7. You can now glue the two sides together, or follow the next few steps to fix the edges together with a fold. Rotate the model 180°.

8. Hold the model at the fold made in Step 6. Keeping both sides of the model together, fold the top points down to the nearest vertical crease.

9. Fold this little flap over once again and turn over.

Slow snail

This paper snail, designed by American origami artist Eric Gjerde, has wonderful proportions and a great folding sequence. Use thin paper if you have some, and you will need a pair of scissors to create the antennae.

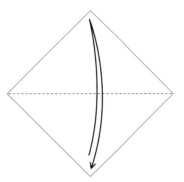

1. Start with a square with the white side up. Fold and unfold in half diagonally.

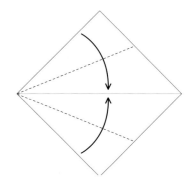

2. Fold both left-hand edges to the central crease.

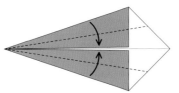

3. Fold both left-hand edges to the central crease once again, leaving a very small gap in the middle.

4. Turn over.

5. Fold both right-hand edges to the central crease.

Skill level: 2

Fold this leaf from scraps of wrapping paper and attach a piece of ribbon to create a simple gift tag.

continued ▶

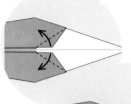

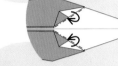

6. Turn over.

7. Mountain fold these two flaps as shown. You may find it easier to valley fold then mountain fold the flaps.

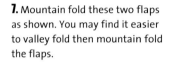

8. Mountain fold along the central crease.

9. Fold the left-hand sides upward together so that they create a 90° angle with the central crease.

10. Unfold.

11. Make the crease made in the previous step a valley fold on both sides. Use both of these creases to bring the left-hand point back up to the 90° angle, as shown in the next diagram.

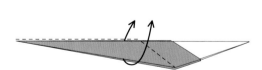

12. Fold the vertical flap down at a 45° angle so that it lies along the central crease.

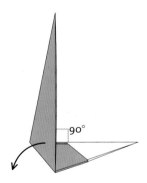

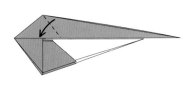

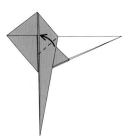

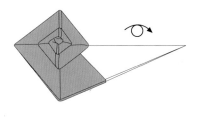

13. Fold the top section down at a 45° angle as shown.

14. Continue to fold this section at 45° angles to the previous fold until you can fold no more. This creates the shell.

15. Once you have completed the spiral, unfold it back to Step 12. Do not flatten the creases you have made, just unwind the spiral. Turn over.

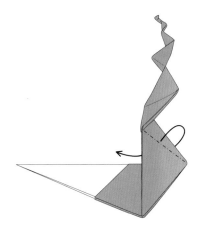

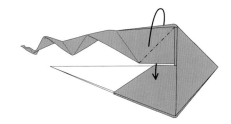

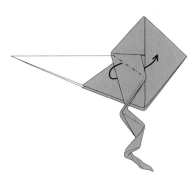

16. Refold the spiral using the existing creases. This time, bring the paper from under itself, as shown in the diagram.

17. Bring the paper over to the front of the body.

18. Continue to create the shell in a counterclockwise fashion. Now the spiral is much tighter and it stays together nicely.

continued ▶

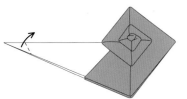

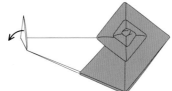

19. Once the shell is completed, fold the left-hand point of the body upward at a 90° angle to create the snail's head.

20. Unfold.

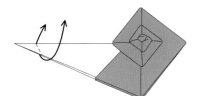

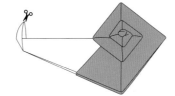

21. Make both creases valley folds and push them upward.

22. Cut along the central part of the head to create two antennae. You can shape them by pinching them slightly between your thumb and index finger.

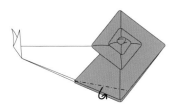

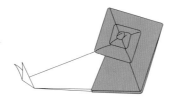

23. Shape the body by folding the bottom part of the shell inside. You may wish to make a valley fold first and then a mountain fold to push the paper under the shell. Repeat on the other side.

These snails won't travel very far, but they will sit nicely on the rim of a plant pot.

Jumping frog

This traditional paper frog is a popular origami model that has been around for a very long time. And yes, it really does jump!

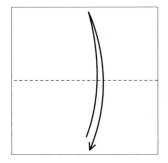

1. Start with a square with the white side up. Fold and unfold in half horizontally.

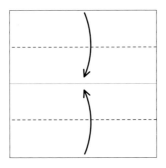

2. Fold the top and bottom raw edges to the central crease.

3. Turn over.

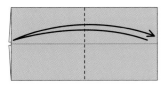

4. Fold the right-hand edge over to the left and unfold.

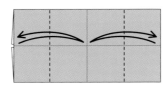

5. Fold and unfold the left- and right-hand raw edges to the central vertical crease. Turn over.

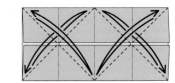

6. Fold and unfold both sets of diagonal creases, as shown.

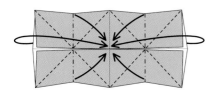

7. Using all the existing creases, bring the left- and right-hand raw edges toward the center of the paper. The paper will collapse as shown in the next step.

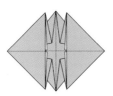

8. Flatten the paper.

Skill level: 2

continued ▶

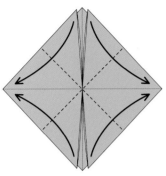

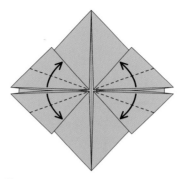

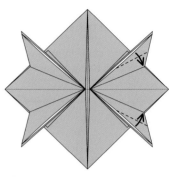

9. Fold the top and bottom left-hand points to the left corner and fold the top and bottom right-hand points to the right corner.

10. Fold all four flaps in half again, as shown.

11. Fold the top and bottom right-hand flaps over to shape the front legs, as shown.

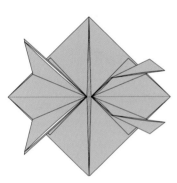

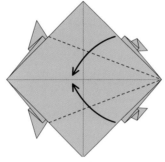

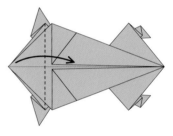

12. Turn over.

13. Fold the top and bottom right-hand edges of the large square to the central horizontal crease.

14. Fold the left-hand corner over to the right. It will land on the central horizontal crease.

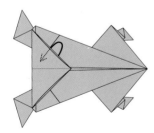

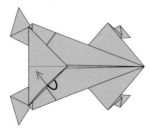

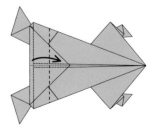

15. Insert the bottom left-hand corner of the top flap into the pocket as shown.

16. Repeat with the bottom flap.

17. Bring the middle of the left-hand vertical edge over to the right-hand corner of the triangle. Flatten and keep in your hand between your thumb and index finger.

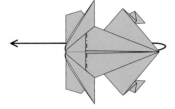

18. Fold the body over to the left, creating a mountain fold in line with the right-hand vertical edge.

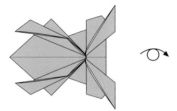

19. Flip the paper over.

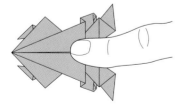

20. Push down on the bottom of the triangle and let go, and your frog will leap into the air.

It's fun to have contests with your friends to see whose frog will jump the farthest.

Little ladybug

No garden is complete without ladybugs. This model, designed by Ioana Stoian, is simple enough that you can use rather small paper. You'll also need a black marker pen. Start by using a 3 x 3 inch (7.5 x 7.5 cm) square but, when you are happy with the folding process, use a square half that size for a more realistic bug.

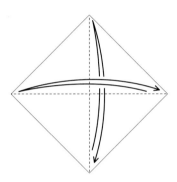

1. Start with a square with the white side up. Fold and unfold both diagonals.

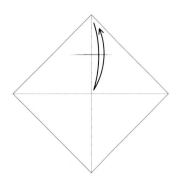

2. Bring the top corner down to the center and pinch the middle. Unfold.

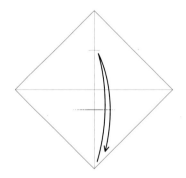

3. Bring the bottom corner up to the pinch mark made in the previous step and make another small pinch as shown. Unfold.

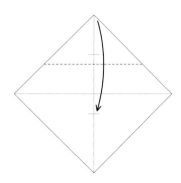

4. Fold the top corner down to this last pinch mark.

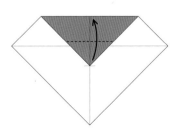

5. Fold this point up to the middle of the top edge.

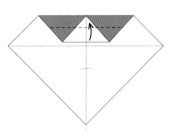

6. Fold this flap in half by bringing the bottom horizontal edge up to the top edge.

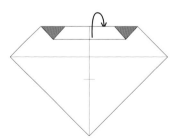

7. Fold this flap over to the other side of the paper using the top horizontal crease.

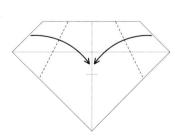

8. Fold the top left- and right-hand diagonal sides to the central vertical crease.

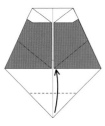

9. Fold the bottom corner up to the bottom edge of these flaps.

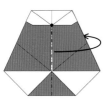

10. Mountain fold along the central crease from the dot down.

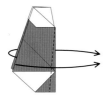

11. Make a valley fold either side of the mountain fold, as shown.

12. Let go of your ladybug.

13. Color in the head with a black marker pen and add some dots.

Paper ladybugs will add a festive note to your next picnic.

Greedy caterpillar

Skill level: 1

Although caterpillars like to eat through the leaves in your garden, they do of course turn into beautiful butterflies. This greedy caterpillar design was created by Ioana Stoian.

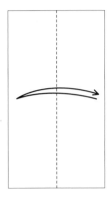

1. Start with a 2:1 rectangle with the white side up. Fold and unfold in half vertically.

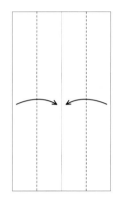

2. Fold the outer edges to the central crease.

3. Fold the bottom edge to the top edge and unfold.

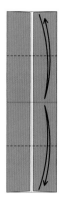

4. Fold the raw edges to the horizontal central crease. Unfold.

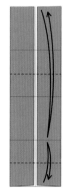

5. Bring the raw edges to the bottom valley fold. Crease and unfold.

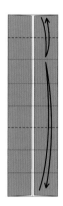

6. Bring the raw edges to the top valley fold. Crease and unfold.

7. Fold and unfold the top corners, as shown.

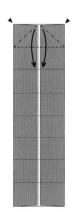

8. Push the corners inward using the folds made in Step 7. The top part should appear as indicated.

9. Pinch the middle of each bottom square.

10. Fold each corner to the nearest pinch mark. The bottom part should appear as shown.

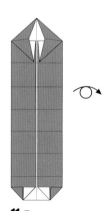

11. Turn over.

12. Starting at the pointed end, fold each mountain fold upward a few millimeters. This will create an accordion-like pleated effect.

13. Mountain fold along the vertical central crease.

14. Fold and unfold the bottom right-hand edge to the existing pinch mark. Rotate the model 90° counterclockwise.

15. Push in the top right-hand corner along the existing creases. This creates the antennae.

16. Gently curve your caterpillar to give it more shape.

Your greedy caterpillar is ready to chomp some leaves. These paper butterflies make pretty brooches.

Striking butterfly

Butterflies have some lovely patterns on their wings, so this project provides the perfect opportunity to use patterned origami paper. This beautiful butterfly was designed by Brazilian origami artist Isa Klein, and is an easy model to remember.

Skill level: 2

See page 26 for instructions for the waterbomb base.

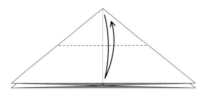

1. Start by folding a waterbomb base with the white side facing out (see Steps 1–4, page 26). Fold the top point down to the bottom edge. Unfold.

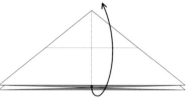

2. Unfold back to a square.

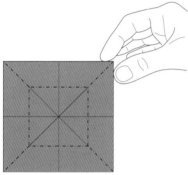

3. Pinch the outer corners together and mountain fold the inner square.

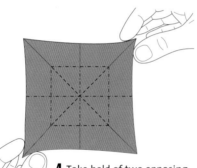

4. Take hold of two opposing corners and gradually pinch them together until they meet in the center. The center of the square will face downward.

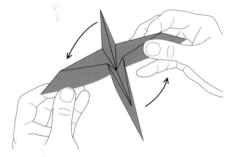

5. Make sure you have two flaps on either side. Now you can lay the model down on the table.

6. Rotate the model 180° so that the longest section is facing upward.

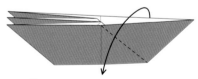

7. Bring the top right-hand flap over to the left.

8. Fold the top right-hand raw edge down to the vertical crease.

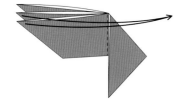

9. Bring two flaps over from the left toward the right.

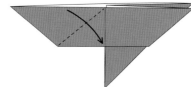

10. Fold the top left-hand raw edge down to the vertical crease.

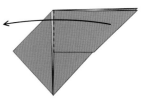

11. Bring the top right-hand flap back over to the left.

12. Mountain fold along the existing vertical crease.

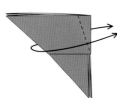

13. Make a diagonal crease as shown and bring both wings toward the right.

14. Crease well and release.

15. Curl the tips of the wings and your butterfly is ready to flutter.

Busy bee

Transporting nectar from one flower to another, bees work ever so hard to make our gardens bloom. This particular bee is a collaborative model by Spanish designer Ángel Écija Blanco and Colombian designer Leyla Torres. You will need a yellow square piece of paper and a black marker pen for this model.

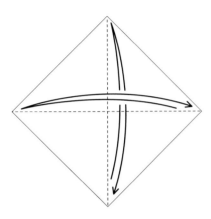

1. Begin with a square with the white side up. Fold and unfold both diagonals.

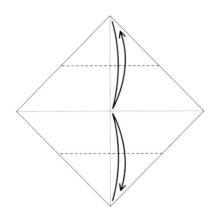

2. Fold the top and bottom corners to the center. Unfold and turn over.

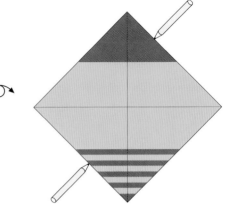

3. Use a black marker pen to color in the top triangular section as shown. For the bottom triangle, draw a series of stripes as shown.

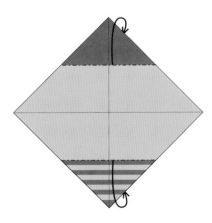

4. Fold these two sections back over to the other side using the existing creases.

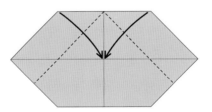

5. Fold the top left- and right-hand horizontal edges down to the central vertical crease.

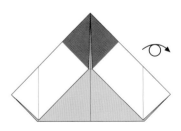

6. Turn over.

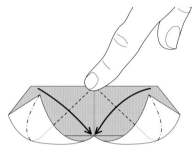

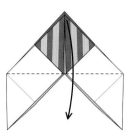

Skill level: 3

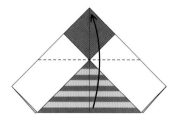

7. Bring the middle of the bottom horizontal edge up to the top point using the existing horizontal valley fold. Hold the top part down with your index finger as shown in the next step.

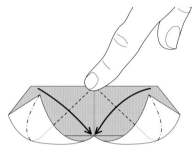

8. Keep your finger on the top area and fold the top left- and right-hand edges down to the central vertical crease, mirroring the back side.

9. Bring the top flap down as far as it will go.

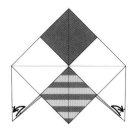

10. Fold the very tips of the wings upward and unfold.

11. Push the wing tips inside using the folds you just made so that they are hidden.

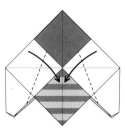

12. Take hold of the bottom part of the right-hand side, including the wing, and fold it over to the central vertical crease. Do not fold through the top black square, but under it—see Step 13 for clarity. Repeat on the left.

continued ▶

13. Mountain fold the tip of the bottom of the top square as shown.

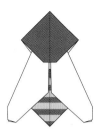

14. Turn over.

15. Now to shape the head. Start by folding the left- and right-hand corners from the top of the wings toward the central crease. Try to make these creases parallel to the central vertical crease.

16. Fold these little flaps back toward the outside at a slight angle as shown.

17. Fold the very tip of these two flaps inward to round off the sharp points.

18. Fold the top point of the head down to the central crease as shown.

19. Fold the top point back up, leaving a very small gap.

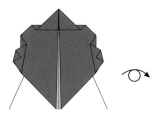

20. Turn over.

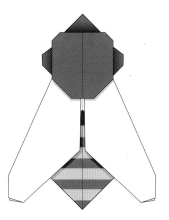

These beautiful bees will be very popular with your friends.

Tasty mushroom

Skill level: 2

Many different types of mushroom grow in the soil—some edible and others poisonous—but at least you don't have to worry with this paper version, designed by Ioana Stoian.

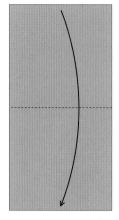

1. Start with a 2:1 rectangle with the colored side up. Fold the top edge down to meet the bottom edge.

2. Bring the bottom raw edge of the top layer back up to the top edge of the paper and make a small pinch mark on either side. Bring the raw edge back down.

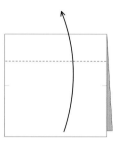

3. Fold the two pinch marks you made in the previous step up to the top horizontal edge.

4. Turn the paper over.

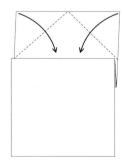

5. Fold the top left- and right-hand corners down to the horizontal edge below.

6. Fold the top point down as shown.

7. Fold the top right-hand corner of the white section down at a 45° angle. Unfold.

8. Squash the right-hand corner down using the previous creases, creating a new crease that runs from the inside point of the existing crease all the way down to the bottom right-hand corner of the paper.

Attach these mushrooms to a piece of string or a long ribbon for some unique summer bunting.

(7–8)

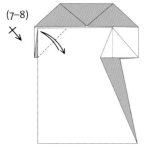

9. Repeat Steps 7–8 on the left.

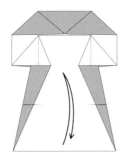

10. Bring the bottom raw edge up to the bottom horizontal flaps and make small pinch marks either side. Bring the raw edge back down.

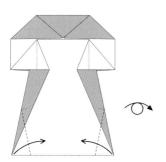

11. Fold the bottom left- and right-hand corners of the paper toward the inside of the mushroom, starting at the pinch marks you just made. Turn over.

Early crocus

Crocuses are the first sign of spring and, if you use the paper size suggested, you really will be surprised at just how realistic this origami version, designed by Ioana Stoian, looks.

Skill level: 2

Learn how to create the square base here.

Note: For best results, use a 3 x 3 inch (7.5 x 7.5 cm) square of paper.

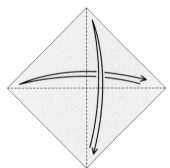

1. Start with a square with the colored side up. Fold and unfold both diagonals. Turn over.

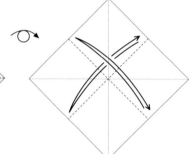

2. Fold and unfold in half in both directions.

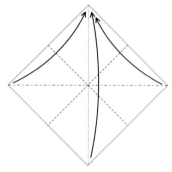

3. Collapse as shown, using all the existing folds.

4. This is the square base with the colored side facing out.

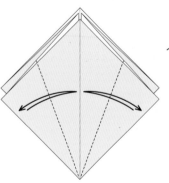

5. Make sure the open edges are facing upward. Fold the bottom left- and right-hand edges of the top layer along the central vertical crease. Unfold and turn over.

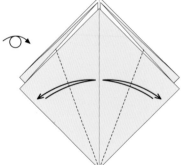

6. Fold the bottom left- and right-hand edges of the top layer along the central vertical crease. Unfold.

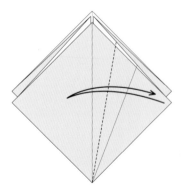

7. Fold the bottom right-hand edge of the top layer over to the existing left-hand valley crease. Unfold.

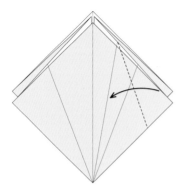

8. Fold the top layer of the right-hand side as shown.

9. Mountain fold the bottom right-hand layer of paper so that it mirrors the top layer, using the section folded in Step 8 as a guide.

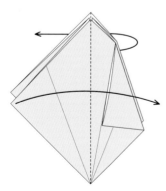

10. Swivel the top left-hand flap over to the right and the bottom right-hand flap over to the left.

Make a simple composition to brighten up your windowsill.

continued ▶

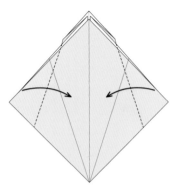

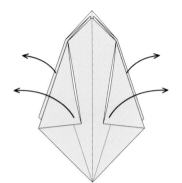

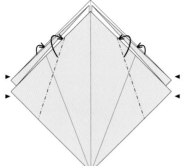

11. Use the back side as a guide to fold the top layer to match.

12. Unfold the creases on both sides back to Step 8.

13. Push all four corners inside the model using the existing creases.

14. Fold the bottom right-hand edge over to the existing crease as shown.

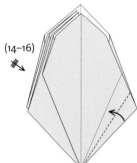

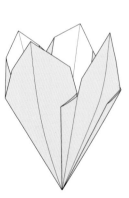

(14–16)

15. Fold this edge over once more, using the existing crease.

16. Fold the top right-hand flap over to the left.

17. Repeat Steps 14–16 on this flap and the two flaps remaining after that. For best results fold all flaps in the same direction.

18. Insert your index finger into the center and open out the flower.

19. Leave the flower as it is or, if you want, you can curl the petals toward the inside of the model.

Crocus leaf

Crocus flowers are often surrounded by leaves. From one square sheet of paper you can fold eight leaves—perfect!

Skill level: 2

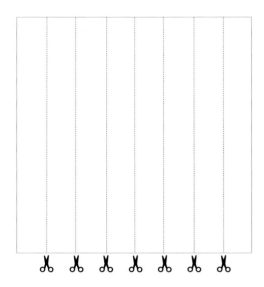

1. Divide a square into eight equal parts and cut into strips. Alternatively, start with an 8:1 rectangle.

2. Start with the white side up. Fold and unfold in half vertically.

3. Bring the left- and right-hand sides to the central vertical crease, but leave a little gap between them.

4. Fold the left- and right-hand sides over once again toward the central crease, leaving a little gap between them.

5. Fold the bottom edge upward. The short part will form the stem and the longer part the leaf.

6. Fold the stem section in half vertically.

7. Shape to your liking. To assemble the flower and stem, cut away the very bottom of the crocus flower and push the flower onto the stem.

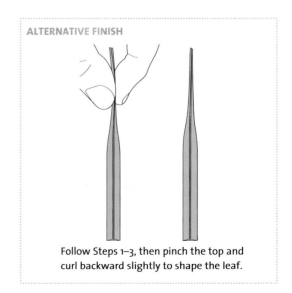

ALTERNATIVE FINISH

Follow Steps 1–3, then pinch the top and curl backward slightly to shape the leaf.

The simplicity of the tulip and stem is an origami classic.

Spring tulip

This tulip is a traditional origami flower with lots of character. Play around with different colored and patterned papers to create your very own variety!

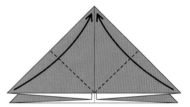

1. Start by folding a waterbomb base with the colored side facing out (see Steps 1–4, page 26). With the open edges at the bottom, fold the bottom left- and right-hand corners of the top flap up to the tip of the triangle.

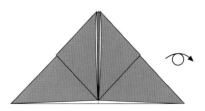

2. Turn over.

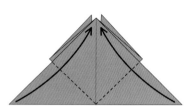

3. Fold the bottom left- and right-hand corners to the top of the triangle.

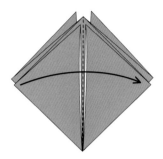

4. Bring the top left-hand flap over to the right using the central vertical crease.

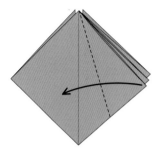

5. Fold the top right-hand flap about ³/₈ inch (1 cm) over the central crease as shown.

Skill level: 2

See page 26 for instructions for the waterbomb base.

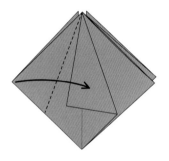

6. Fold the left-hand flap about ³/₈ inch (1 cm) over the central crease as shown.

7. Turn over.

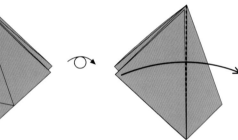

8. Bring the top left-hand flap over to the right.

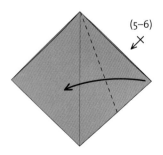

9. Repeat Steps 5–6 on this side using the back side as a guide.

(5–6)

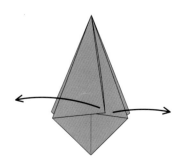

10. Open out both flaps slightly.

continued ▶

11. Insert the right-hand flap into the pocket of the left-hand flap.

12. Turn over.

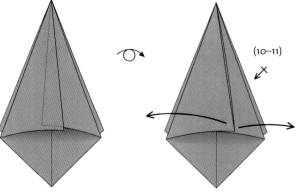

(10–11)

13. Repeat Steps 10–11 on this side.

14. Rotate the model 180°.

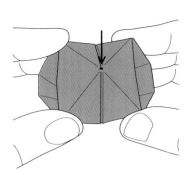

15. Hold the model as shown and inflate the flower by blowing into the little hole.

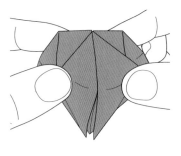

16. Rotate the flower 180° so that it's facing the right way up.

17. Gently peel back all four petals.

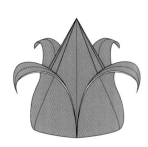

Tulip stem

The origami tulip (see pages 56–58) makes a gorgeous display when paired with this relatively simple stem.

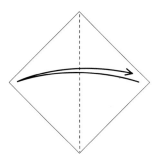

1. Start with a square with the white side up. Fold and unfold in half diagonally.

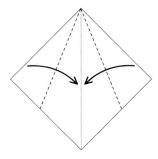

2. Fold the top left- and right-hand edges down along the central crease.

3. Fold the bottom left- and right-hand edges up along the central crease.

4. Fold the bottom left- and right-hand edges up along the central vertical crease once again.

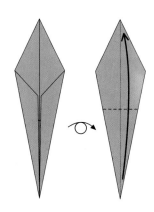

5. Turn over.

6. Fold the bottom point up to the top point.

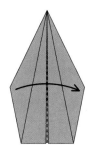

7. Fold the left-hand side over to the right using the central crease.

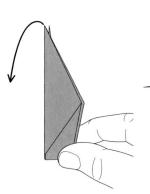

8. Keep the base pinched between your thumb and index finger. Use the other hand to peel the outer layer downward, creating the leaf.

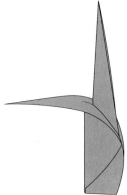

9. You can now insert the spike into the hole at the bottom of the tulip.

Stylized carnation

This unique flower, designed by Ioana Stoian, would look beautiful on a greeting card.

Skill level: 2

See page 26 for instructions for the waterbomb base.

Note: For best results, use a 3 x 3 inch (7.5 x 7.5 cm) square of solid-colored paper.

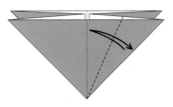

1. Start by folding a waterbomb base with the colored side facing out (see Steps 1–4, page 26). With the open edges at the top, fold the bottom edge of the top right-hand flap over to the central vertical crease. Unfold.

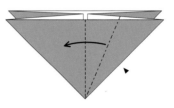

2. Insert your index finger into the top of this flap and, using the creases created in the previous step, push up on the bottom right-hand edge and squash the flap down.

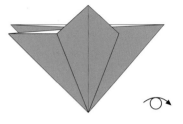

3. Turn over.

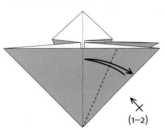

4. Repeat Steps 1–2 on this side.

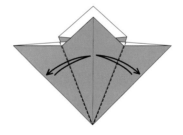

5. Fold and unfold the left- and right-hand bottom edges to the central vertical crease.

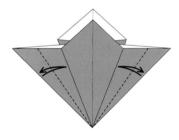

6. Fold and unfold the left- and right-hand bottom edges as shown.

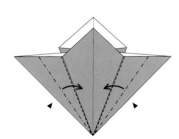

7. Repeat the same action as Step 2, pushing up on the bottom edges to squash these two flaps down.

8. Turn over.

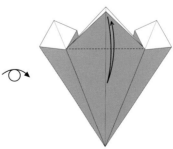

9. Fold the tip of the triangle of the top layer down as far as it will go. Unfold.

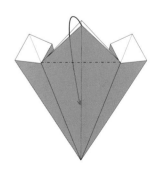

10. Insert this triangular flap toward the inside of the model, covering all the inside edges. This will "lock" the flower together.

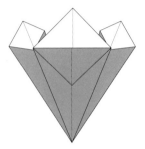

11. Turn over.

12. Curl the tips of the petals outward.

The inside pocket provides an excellent place to hide a secret note.

Carnation stem

You can make a stem that fits perfectly with the carnation flower (see pages 60–61), creating a wonderful ensemble.

Note: If you used a 3 x 3 inch (7.5 x 7.5 cm) square for your flower, try folding the stem from a 1¹⁄₂ x 6 inch (3.75 x 15 cm) rectangle.

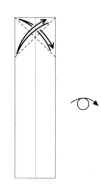

1. Divide a square into four equal pieces and cut along the crease marks. Alternatively, begin with a 4:1 rectangle.

2. With the white side facing up, fold and unfold in half lengthwise.

3. Fold and unfold the top right-hand corner down to the left-hand edge and the top left-hand corner down to the right-hand edge as shown. Turn over.

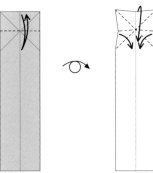

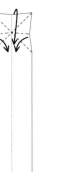

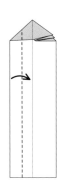

4. Fold the top edge down so that it goes through the intersection of both diagonals. Unfold and turn over.

5. Collapse this top section using all the existing creases, as shown.

6. Flatten and bring the left-hand side of the top triangular flap to the right.

7. Fold the left-hand raw edge to the central vertical crease.

8. Fold the left-hand edge over to the central vertical crease once again.

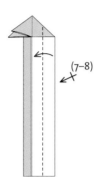
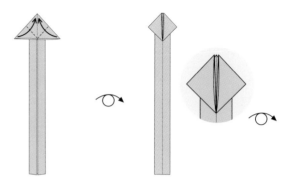

(7–8)

9. Bring both triangular flaps from the right over to the left.

10. Repeat Steps 7–8 on the right-hand side.

11. Bring the top left-hand triangle back over to the right. The result will be an arrow shape.

12. Fold both bottom corners of the triangle up to the top point. Turn over.

13. Fold the top point down along the central crease as shown. Turn over.

14. Now you are ready to attach the stem to your flower.

ASSEMBLING THE CARNATION

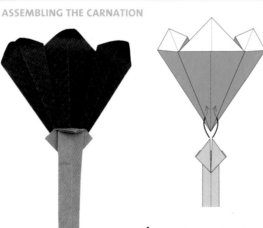
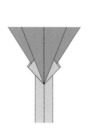
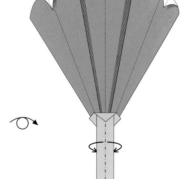

1. Take the carnation head and the stem with the reverse sides facing up, and insert the two flaps of the stem under the top triangular flap of the flower.

2. Push the flaps up as far as they will go and turn the paper over.

3. Pinch both sides of the stem together, making a mountain fold all the way up. Then shape the bottom part as you like.

Pretty flower

This traditional flower looks best folded from double-sided paper. You can fold the petals flat, creating a very angular flower, or curl them gently for a more organic look.

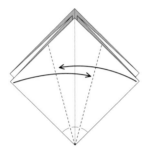

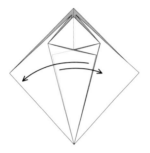

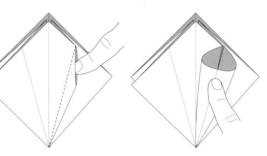

Skill level: 3

See page 52 for instructions for the square base.

1. Start by folding a square base with the white side facing out (see Steps 1–4, page 52). With the open flaps at the top, starting at the bottom point, fold the top right-hand flap over to the left and the top left-hand flap over to the right to create three equal sections. Flatten.

2. Unfold the left-hand flap all the way back, but only unfold the right-hand flap halfway, so that it stands upright.

3. Insert your index finger into the small pocket at the top of this flap.

4. Flatten the pocket evenly, aligning the existing crease with the edge of paper behind it. The left-hand side of the pocket should meet up with the main central fold.

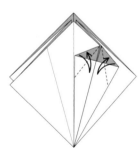

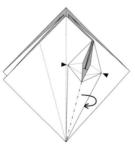

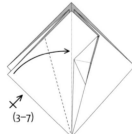

5. Fold and unfold the left- and right-hand sides of this small section to the central crease as shown.

6. Lift up the horizontal edge of the paper and, using the previous creases, fold it down as far as it will go. This will create a new point that lies on the central crease.

7. Flatten this section. Mountain fold along the existing middle crease so that the right-hand side disappears behind the left.

8. Fold the top left-hand flap toward the center and repeat Steps 3–7, but fold the left-hand edge under the right instead.

9. Turn over.

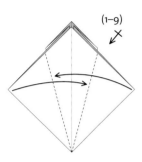

10. Use the back side as a guide to fold this section into three equal parts. Repeat Steps 1–9 on this side.

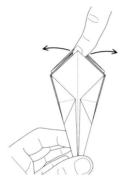

11. Holding the base between your thumb and index finger, insert your other index finger into the center to open up the cone.

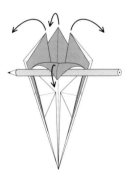

12. Use a pen or pencil to curl the petals as far as they will go.

Use double-sided paper for the best results.

Dainty bellflower

Bellflowers exist in many shapes, colors, and sizes. This traditional model looks best when it is attached to a piece of wire so that it can dance in the wind.

Skill level: 3

See page 52 for instructions for the square base.

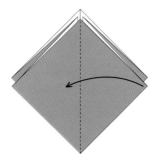

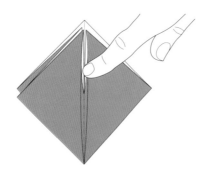

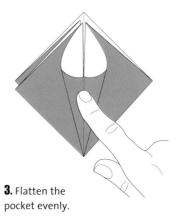

1. Start by folding a square base with the colored side facing out (see Steps 1–4, page 52). With the open flaps facing upward, bring the top right-hand flap over toward the left so that it stands up vertically.

2. Insert your index finger into the pocket and squash down, aligning the vertical crease with the edges behind it.

3. Flatten the pocket evenly.

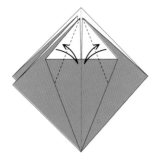

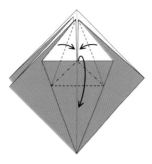

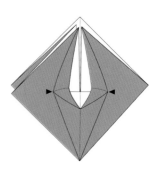

4. Fold the top left- and right-hand sides of this section to the central crease, starting from the top point. Unfold.

5. Lift up the horizontal edge of paper and, using the previous creases, fold it down as far as it will go. This will create a new point that lies on the middle crease as shown.

6. Flatten.

This is an elegant paper flower that looks good in any color.

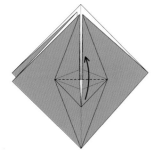

7. Fold the small triangle upward as far as it will go.

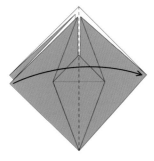

8. Bring the top large left-hand flap over toward the right using the central vertical crease.

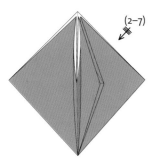

9. Repeat Steps 2–7 on this flap and then on the remaining two large flaps.

10. Pull on two opposing spikes and open the model slightly.

continued ▶

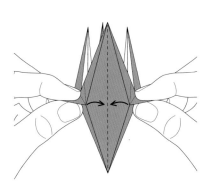

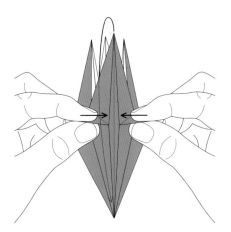

11. Take hold of two small consecutive triangles, with your index finger on the top and thumb underneath, holding the triangles flat. Bring the triangles together and the spike in between will naturally fold along its vertical crease, creating a tight join.

12. Still keeping hold of the small triangles, fold the spike inside the model as far as it will go.

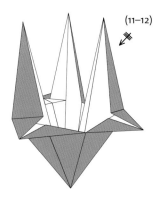

(11–12)

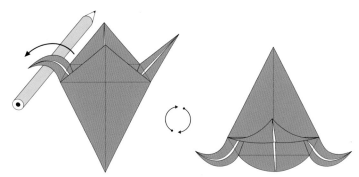

13. You'll be left with the two triangles joined together at the base. Repeat Steps 11–12 on the remaining three spikes.

14. Curl the tips of the triangles outward to create the petals. Rotate the model 180°.

Wire stems have been added to these blooms to create a beautiful bouquet.

Skill level: 3
See page 52 for instructions for the square base.

Fragrant lily

This paper lily is a very popular and well-known traditional origami flower. Attach the flower to a wire stem and fold a few more to build up a beautiful bouquet.

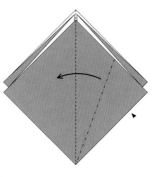

1. Start by folding a square base with the colored side facing out (see Steps 1–4, page 52). With the open flaps facing upward, fold and unfold the bottom right-hand edge of the top flap to the central crease.

2. Insert your index finger into the top of the flap and, using the creases made in the previous step, push up on the bottom edge.

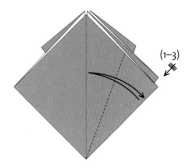

3. Flatten and turn over.

4. Repeat Steps 1–3 on the remaining three flaps.

continued ▶

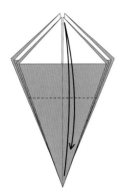

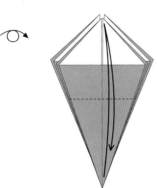

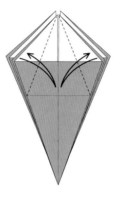

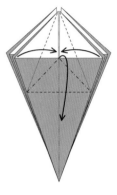

5. Fold the bottom point up to the top point. Unfold and turn over.

6. Fold the bottom point up to the top point and unfold.

7. Fold and unfold the top left- and right-hand edges of the top layer of paper down along the central crease.

8. Bring the horizontal edge down along the central crease using the existing creases. This will cause the top left- and right-hand edges to meet.

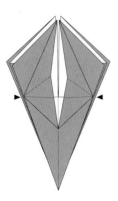

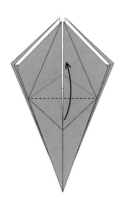

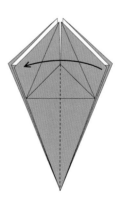

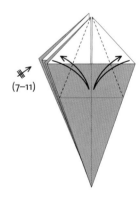

9. Flatten.

10. Fold the little triangular flap upward.

11. Bring the next large right-hand flap over to the left, using the central vertical crease.

12. Repeat Steps 7–11 on the three remaining flaps.

Double-sided sparkly paper makes these flowers look very chic.

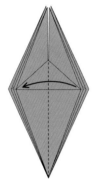

13. Bring the top right-hand flap over to the left so that you have a diamond shape.

14. Fold the bottom left- and right-hand edges of the top layer up along the vertical crease.

15. Bring the next large flap from the right-hand side over to the left, using the central vertical fold.

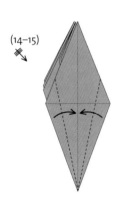

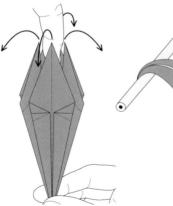

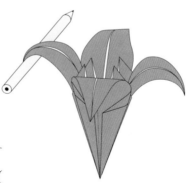

(14–15)

16. Repeat Steps 14–15 on all three remaining flaps.

17. Insert your index finger into the center to open out the lily.

18. Shape the petals by curling them out using a pen or pencil.

Flower in full bloom

This contemporary flower, designed by Ioana Stoian, is very versatile. Use the little tip at the back to attach it to a branch, turn it into a brooch, or stick it onto a nicely wrapped gift!

Skill level: 2

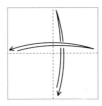

1. Start with a square with the white side up. Fold and unfold in half in both directions.

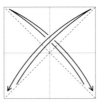

2. Fold and unfold both diagonals. Turn over.

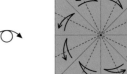

3. Fold and unfold each section between the existing creases in half, making sure that every line goes through the center of the square.

4. Mountain fold along the central vertical crease.

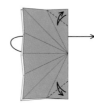

5. Fold the top and bottom right-hand edges to meet their closest diagonal creases. Unfold back to Step 4.

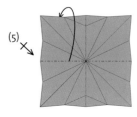

6. Mountain fold along the horizontal central crease and repeat Step 5.

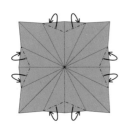

7. Press on the center so the sides pop up. Push in the middle of each of the four sides so the creases become mountain folds. The paper will no longer lie flat.

8. Rotate the model by 45°.

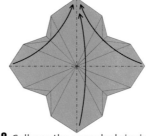

9. Collapse the paper by bringing all the mountain folds to the central vertical crease.

10. Fold the bottom point about one-fifth of the way up. Crease well.

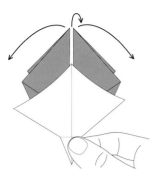

11. Holding the folded-up tip, use a finger to press down firmly in the center of the flower and open up the petals.

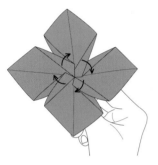

12. Still holding the tip, lay each inside flap along the crease in the middle of the nearest petal. All flaps should follow the same direction.

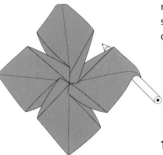

13. Curl the petal tips back slightly using a pen or pencil.

Slip the back of this flower under the middle of the Decorative leaf (see page 32) for a nice ensemble.

Proud crow

Always planning ahead, crows are among the most intelligent animals in the world. This traditional crow is so clever it can perch all by itself.

Skill level: 2

See page 52 for instructions for the square base.

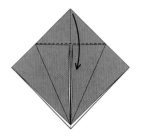

1. Start by folding a square base with the colored side facing out (see Steps 1–4, page 52). With the open flaps facing downward, fold the bottom left- and right-hand edges of the top flaps to the vertical crease.

2. Fold the top point down across the top of the existing flaps.

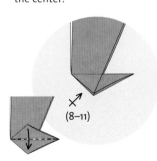

3. Unfold all three flaps.

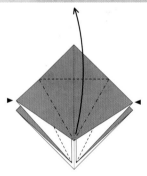

4. Lift the top layer of paper up as far as it will go, while at the same time pushing the raw edges toward the center.

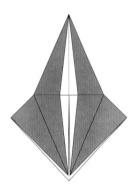

5. Turn over.

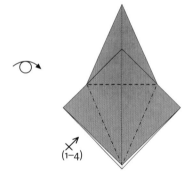

6. Repeat Steps 1–4 on this side.

7. Fold both bottom points up to the center.

8. Now to focus on the feet. For the first foot, fold the inside edge down to the bottom edge.

9. Fold back up.

10. Insert your index finger between the flaps and squash flat using the previous creases.

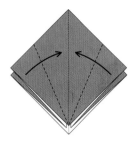

11. Fold the top half down to complete the foot. Repeat Steps 8–11 for the other foot.

12. Fold down the top flap of the main part of the model along the existing horizontal crease.

13. Mountain fold the entire model along the central vertical crease.

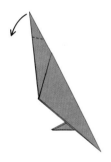

14. Now focus on the head. Fold the top point down at the angle of your choice.

15. Unfold.

16. Push the head inside so that the beak sticks out.

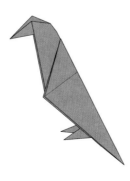

Experiment with your paper choices. Different patterns can lead to very different results.

Hungry pigeon

There always seems to be at least one large pigeon looking for food in the garden. This traditional bird is fun to fold and makes a sweet table decoration.

Skill level: 2

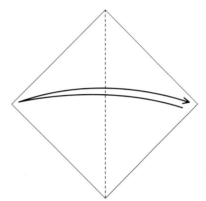

1. Start with a square with the white side up. Fold and unfold in half diagonally.

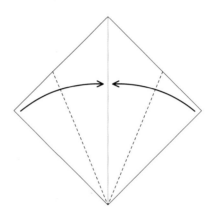

2. Fold the bottom raw edges to the central crease.

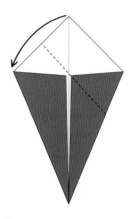

3. Fold the top point to the left-hand corner: the right-hand corner will land on the vertical crease made in Step 1.

4. Unfold.

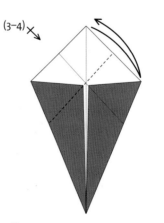

5. Repeat Steps 3–4 from the opposite side. Turn over.

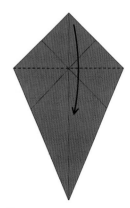

6. Fold the tip of the model down as far as it will go.

7. Turn over.

8. Open out the right-hand side.

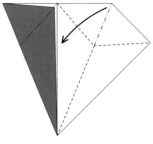

9. Bring the top right-hand edge down to the vertical crease using the existing creases, and collapse the right-hand raw edge along the central fold.

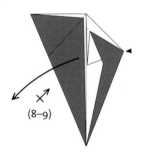

10. Flatten and repeat Steps 8–9 on the left-hand side.

11. Fold the flaps down as far as they will go.

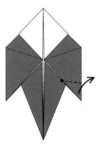

12. Fold the tip of the right-hand flap from around ³⁄₈ inch (1 cm) under the central intersection so that the double raw edge is parallel to the crease above it.

13. Fold in half vertically.

14. Fold the bottom point of the remaining flap to mirror the fold made in Step 12.

15. Fold the bottom point up as shown.

continued ▶

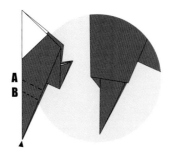

16. Leave ³/₈ inch (1 cm) from the bottom and fold the tip back down.

17. Unfold Steps 15 and 16.

18. Make crease A into a mountain fold and crease B into a valley fold. Use the creases to push the tail inside the body.

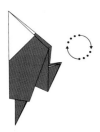

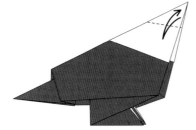

19. Rotate the model 90° clockwise.

20. Make a fold as shown to form the head, and unfold.

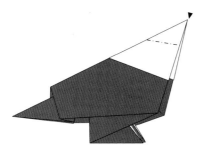

21. Push the head inside so that the beak sticks out.

The fish scales on the paper make very interesting feathers for this pigeon.

Jenny wren

This beautiful wren is designed by Viviane Berty, a French origami folder. It stands firmly on its two feet and the tips of the wings provide extra support.

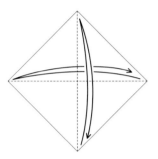

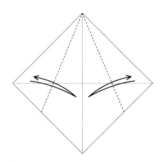

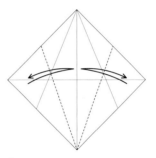

1. Start with a square with the white side up. Fold and unfold both diagonals.

2. Fold the top raw edges to the central vertical crease. Unfold.

3. Repeat Step 2 with the bottom raw edges.

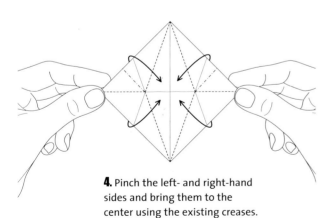

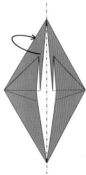

4. Pinch the left- and right-hand sides and bring them to the center using the existing creases.

5. Mountain fold along the central vertical crease.

6. Fold the bottom point up to the top point.

7. Fold the top left-hand edge along the bottom edge. Unfold.

continued ▶

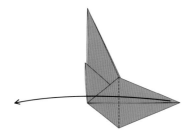

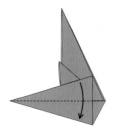

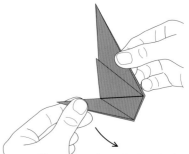

8. Insert your index finger into the pocket and squash it down symmetrically.

9. Fold the right-hand point over to the left as far as it will go.

10. Fold the top half down along the existing crease.

11. Keeping the right-hand side together with your right hand, use your left hand to swivel the left-hand point down slightly.

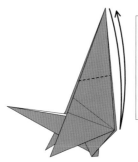

The tips of the wren's wings help it to stand up.

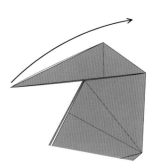

12. Fold the front and back flaps down on either side of the body.

13. Now that your bird can stand on its own two feet, let's focus on shaping the head. Fold the top point down as shown. Unfold.

14. Fold the top point down from the left-hand side of the previous crease until the right-hand edge crosses the dot.

15. Unfold.

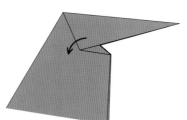

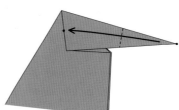

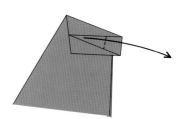

16. Insert your index finger into the pocket and lower the tip down using the existing creases.

17. Flatten the head.

18. Fold the tip of the beak to the middle of the head.

19. Fold the tip back to the right, making a crease parallel to the previous fold.

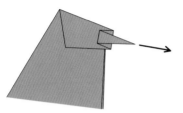

20. Unfold Steps 18 and 19.

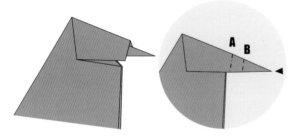

A B

21. Make crease A into a mountain fold and crease B into a valley fold. Use the creases to push the beak inside the head.

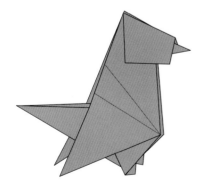

For an alternative look, try paper with a nice, bold print.

Night owls

These owls, designed by English origami creator Wayne Brown, are full of character. You can even fold a branch for them to perch on while they visit your garden at night.

Skill level: 3

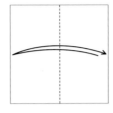

1. Start with a square with the white side up. Fold and unfold in half vertically.

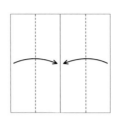

2. Fold both outer edges to the central crease.

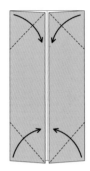

3. Fold the four corners to the central crease.

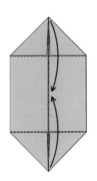

4. Fold the top and bottom points over the flaps of paper so that they meet in the center.

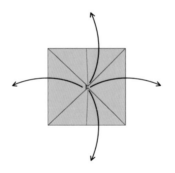

5. Unfold completely.

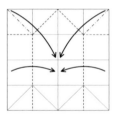

6. Bring the top corners down to the central crease using the existing diagonal creases. Both outer edges will naturally come toward the central crease. Press down flat.

7. Fold the top edges of these two flaps down to the outside edges.

8. Bring the bottom inside corners of the top layer of paper up to the center, using the existing creases. Both bottom edges will now lie on the central vertical fold.

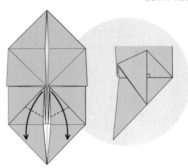

9. Fold both points down to the diagonal edge, creating a 90° angle with the existing horizontal crease.

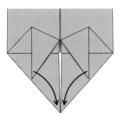

10. Bring both points down to the bottom point.

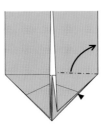

11. Bring the horizontal crease on the right-hand side of the model to the outside edge, without flattening the paper.

12. Bring the corner downward using the existing creases (see next diagram).

13. Bring the inside edge back to the central crease.

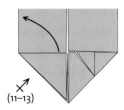

(11–13)

14. Repeat Steps 11–13 on the left-hand side.

15. Fold the bottom point up to the bottom of the flaps.

16. Turn over.

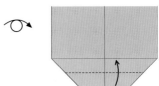

17. Fold the bottom edge up to the existing horizontal crease, allowing the triangle behind to swing to the front.

18. Make two folds as shown.

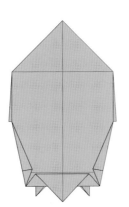

19. Turn over.

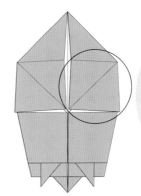

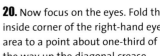

20. Now focus on the eyes. Fold the inside corner of the right-hand eye area to a point about one-third of the way up the diagonal crease.

continued ▶

21. Fold the small diagonal edge upward as shown.

22. Fold along the diagonal crease as indicated.

23. Fold this point down, creating a small right-angled triangle.

(20–24)

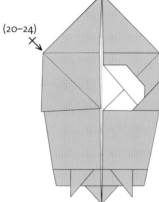

24. Fold this little diagonal edge over, using the existing central diagonal crease.

25. Repeat Steps 20–24 for the left eye.

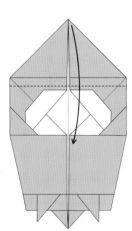

26. Fold the top point down past the bottom of the eyes. This will create a new horizontal crease.

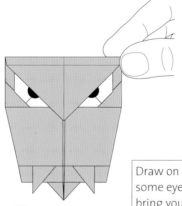

27. Use your thumb and index finger to shape the top of the head and the tip of the beak.

Draw on some eyes to bring your owl to life.

Place an owl on your desk and it may just share some of its wisdom with you.

Perching branch

The owl's branch, also designed by Wayne Brown, is a simple model to fold. It can be used to support other origami creatures too.

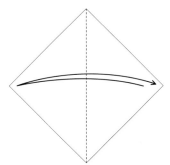

1. Start with a square with the white side up. Fold and unfold in half diagonally.

2. Bring the bottom corner to the left-hand corner and make a small pinch of about 1 inch (2.5 cm) in length. Unfold.

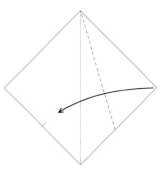

3. Fold the right-hand corner over to the pinch mark, starting the fold at the top point.

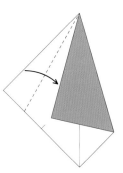

4. Bring the left-hand raw edge to meet the raw edge of the previous fold.

5. Fold through the join so that the left-hand edge aligns with the central crease.

6. Bring the top point to the bottom point and make a small pinch in the middle. Unfold and rotate the model 90° counterclockwise.

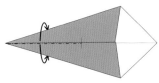

7. Mountain fold from point to pinch mark.

Skill level: 3

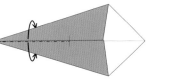

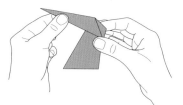

8. Holding the left-hand side firmly, use the pinch mark as a pivot to swing the right-hand corner down toward your left hand.

9. When you are happy with the angle, pinch the right-hand sides together.

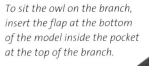

To sit the owl on the branch, insert the flap at the bottom of the model inside the pocket at the top of the branch.

Pair of pants

These simple pants are based on a traditonal model that has been very slightly modified by Ioana Stoian. They would be great for greeting cards and summer decorations.

Skill level: 1

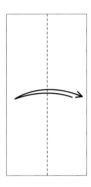

1. Start with a 2:1 rectangle, with the white side up. Fold and unfold in half vertically.

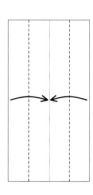

2. Fold the left- and right-hand raw edges to the central crease.

3. Turn over.

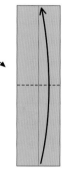

4. Fold the bottom raw edge to the top raw edge.

5. Fold both bottom corners up to the central crease. Unfold back to Step 3.

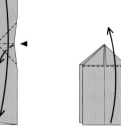

6. Using the existing creases, push the sides toward the center and bring the top edge to meet the bottom edge.

7. Fold the bottom raw edge of the top flap up as shown.

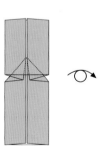

8. Turn over.

Note: To make items of clothing in proportion to one another, use the following guideline to create a whole outfit from one square of paper. **A** = Pants, **B** = Shirt, **C** and **D** = Underpants

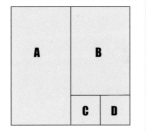

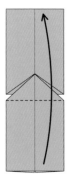 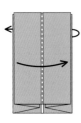 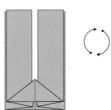

9. Fold the bottom raw edge to meet the top raw edge.

10. Fold the left-hand side of the top flap over to the right and repeat on the back.

11. Rotate the paper 180°.

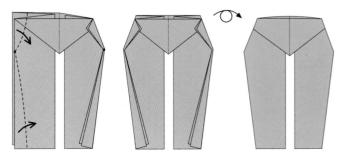

12. Imagine a dot on the edge of the right pants leg in line with the bottom of the triangle. Fold both flaps of the paper in two places from this dot to taper the waist and leg. Repeat on the left pants leg. Turn over.

Simple underpants

This very simple model, designed by Ioana Stoian, will add a bit of humor to your clothes line.

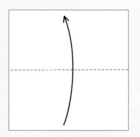 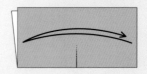

1. Start with a square with the white side up. Fold in half horizontally.

2. Bring the left-hand edge to the right-hand edge and pinch along the bottom edge only. Unfold.

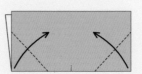 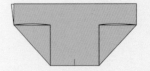

3. Using the central pinch to guide your eye, fold both corners symmetrically upward.

4. Turn over.

Skill level: 1

Short-sleeved shirt

Fold a summery shirt to go with the trendy pants on pages 86–87.
This traditional model is simple, fun, and works well with a dollar bill.

Skill level: 1

Soon you'll have a miniature closet full of origami clothes.

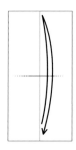

1. Start with a 2:1 rectangle, with the white side up. Fold and unfold in half vertically.

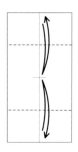

2. Bring the bottom edge up to the top edge and pinch at the center. Unfold.

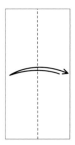

3. Fold and unfold the top and bottom raw edges to the pinch mark.

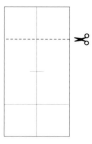

4. Cut along the top crease.

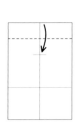

5. Fold the top raw edge down to the pinch mark, aligning along the vertical crease.

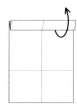

6. Fold the bottom edge of the flap back up to the top edge.

7. Fold the bottom edge of the flap up again.

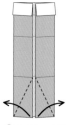

8. Fold the left- and right-hand edges to the central vertical crease.

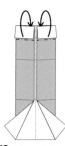

9. Fold out the bottom corners as shown.

10. Mountain fold the top section along the existing crease.

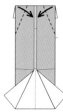

11. Fold the top left- and right-hand corners to the central vertical crease to an imaginary point about ¼ inch (0.5 cm) down.

12. Fold the bottom edge up and slide it under the collar. Flatten.

Smart socks

This cute pair of socks, designed by Ioana Stoian, will take only a few minutes to make. Transform them into Christmas stockings with red and white paper.

Skill level: 1

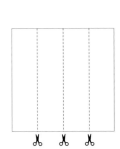

1. Fold a square into four equal sections and cut along the creases.

2. Take one of the resulting rectangles with the colored side up. Fold and unfold in half horizontally.

3. Bring the top edge to the central crease and make a pinch mark at the right-hand edge only. Unfold.

4. Fold the bottom edge to the pinch mark. Unfold and turn over.

5. Bring the right-hand edge to the left-hand edge and make a pinch mark in the center of the bottom edge. Unfold.

6. Fold the bottom corners up to meet the pinch mark.

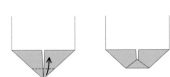

7. Fold the tip of the resulting triangle one-third of the way back up.

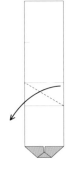

8. Make a fold as shown.

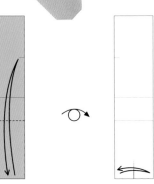

9. Fold the paper back on itself along the existing crease.

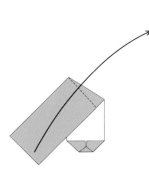

10. Fold the corner in the center up—it will line up with the horizontal crease on the other side of the model.

11. Turn over.

12. Make two small folds to form the cuff and the heel, as shown.

Follow the instructions to make a second sock, but at Step 8, fold on the opposite diagonal to complete the pair.

PROJECTS

Summer dress

American origami designer Alison Riesel created this very fashionable origami dress. Hang it on the clothes line along with the other items of clothing, or use it to embellish a greeting card.

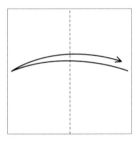

1. Begin with a square with the white side up. Fold in half and unfold.

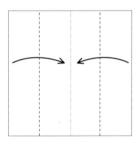

2. Fold both outer edges to the central crease.

3. Turn over.

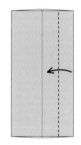

4. Bring the right-hand edge to the central crease, allowing the bottom flap to swing to the front.

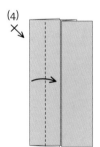

5. Repeat Step 4 on the left-hand side.

6. Turn over.

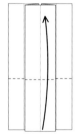

7. Fold the bottom edge upward, leaving a finger's width space from the top edge.

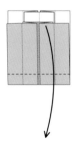

8. Fold this flap downward, forming the crease a finger's width space from the bottom.

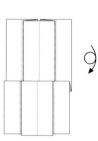

9. Flip the model over so the colored side is facing upward and the longest section is downward.

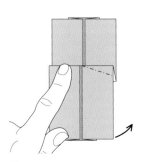

(10)

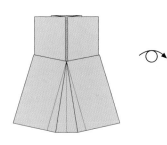

10. Press down on the left-hand side and swivel the bottom right-hand corner upward as far as it will go. Flatten.

11. Repeat Step 10 on the left-hand side. Flatten.

12. Turn over.

13. Fold the top edges of the middle flap down along the central crease. Unfold.

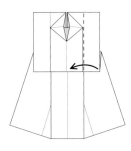

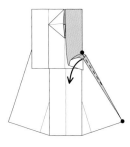

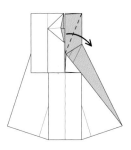

14. Pull the top layer down so that the top edges meet along the central crease, squashing the triangles.

15. Bring the bottom right-hand corner over to the central crease, and fold. Note that the flap will not lie flat.

16. Create a fold between the two dots so that the model becomes flat.

17. Fold the inside edge of the bodice outward following the dotted line.

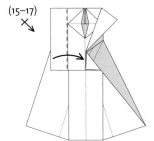

(15–17)

18. Repeat Steps 15–17 on the left-hand side of the dress.

19. Fold both central corners on the diagonal to create the neckline. Experiment with various angles to obtain different-looking dresses.

20. Turn over.

Spinning pinwheel

This is a simple, traditional model that can also be used in your "real" garden. You'll need a stick or a pencil and a pushpin, so that your pinwheel can spin in the wind.

Skill level: 1

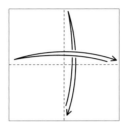

1. Start with a square with the white side up. Fold and unfold in half in both directions.

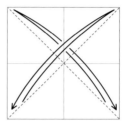

2. Fold and unfold both diagonals.

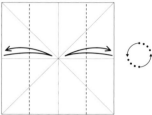

3. Fold the left- and right-hand raw edges to the central vertical crease. Unfold. Rotate 90°.

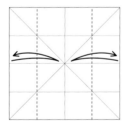

4. Fold the left- and right-hand raw edges to the central vertical crease. Unfold.

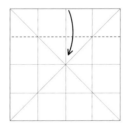

5. Bring the middle of the top edge down to the center of the square using the existing folds.

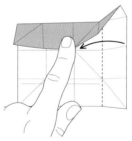

6. Hold this down with your index finger and bring the middle of the right-hand edge to the center.

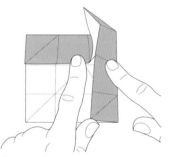

7. The two sides should come together as shown. Flatten.

8. Rotate 90° counterclockwise.

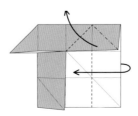

9. Bring the middle of the right-hand edge to the center as you did in Step 6.

10. Flatten the paper once again and rotate 90° counterclockwise.

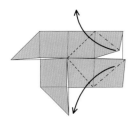

11. Bring the middle of the right-hand edge to the center once again. This time you will create two arms at the same time.

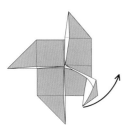

12. Flatten the remaining arms, making sure they all go in the same direction.

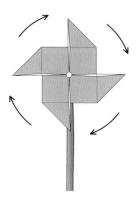

13. Insert a pushpin through the center of the pinwheel and into a pencil or stick.

This model is a fun way to upcycle old giftwrap.

Mini watering can

Although this watering can can't actually hold any water, it makes a very cute decoration. Created by Ioana Stoian, this model is a must in your origami garden.

Skill level: 3

See page 52 for instructions for the square base.

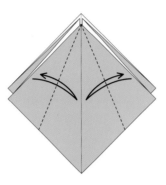

1. Start by folding a square base with the colored side facing out (see Steps 1–4, page 52). With the open flaps facing upward, fold the top left- and right-hand flaps to the central vertical crease. Unfold.

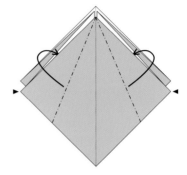

2. Push the paper to the inside of the flap using the previous creases.

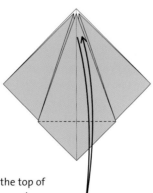

3. Fold the top of this diamond shape down as far as it will go, and unfold. Turn over.

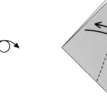

4. Repeat Steps 1–3 on this side.

(1–3)

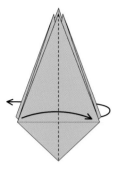

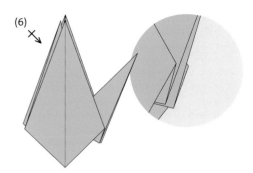

5. Swivel the top left-hand flap over to the right and the bottom right-hand flap over to the left.

6. Take hold of the middle right-hand section and pull it downward until the long edge aligns with the short hinge created. Refer to the next illustration for clarity.

7. Repeat Step 6 on the left-hand side.

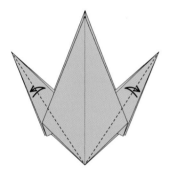

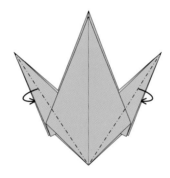

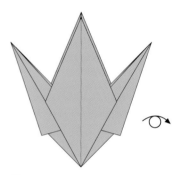

8. Fold a crease that links the bottom point and the top of the right-hand spike. Only fold the top section of paper. Unfold and repeat on the left-hand side.

9. Push the paper toward the inside of the left-and right-hand spikes, using the previously made creases.

10. Turn over.

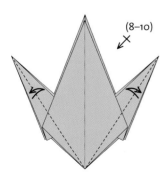

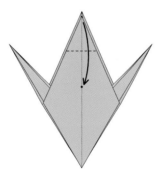

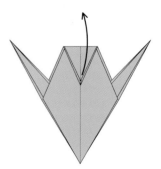

11. Repeat Steps 8–10 on this side.

12. Fold both tips down along the central crease so that they match up with the start of the left- and right-hand "spikes."

13. Unfold the top layer.

continued ▶

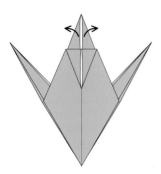

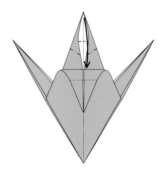

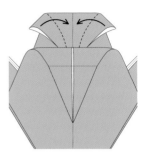

14. Slightly open the back flap as shown.

15. Bring the front flap down toward you a little so it is out of the way. Fold the tip of the back section down along the existing horizontal crease.

16. Fold the left- and right-hand sides of this section back to the central vertical crease, using the existing creases.

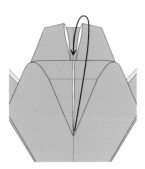

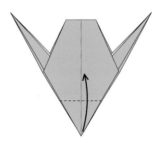

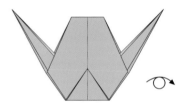

17. Insert the triangle of the front flap into the pocket you have just made.

18. Fold the bottom point upward to the central crease as far as it goes without strain. This flap will be used to make your finished watering can stand up by itself.

19. Turn over.

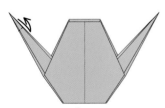

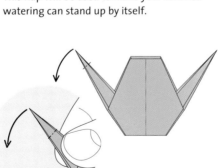

20. Fold and unfold the tip of the left-hand spike about one-third of the way down.

21. Pinch the spike just underneath the crease made in the previous step. Bring the tip down using the existing crease.

22. Keeping the bottom part of the spike pinched in one hand, use the other hand to gently peel back the outer layers of paper to create the spout.

23. Fold the tip of the right-hand spike over to the left, as shown. Unfold.

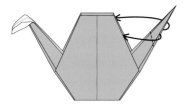

24. Use the creases created in the previous step to reverse the paper and push the tip of the spike inside the body of the watering can.

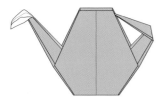

25. Hide the tip inside the body of the watering can.

You could use these watering cans as place cards at a summer party.

Miniature trowel

This cute little trowel, designed by Ioana Stoian, will make a great gift for a green-fingered friend.

TO MAKE THE BLADE

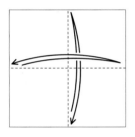

1. Start with a square with the white side up. Fold and unfold in half in both directions. Turn over.

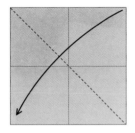

2. Bring the top right-hand corner down to the bottom left-hand corner.

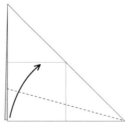

3. Fold the bottom edge upward, starting from the right-hand point, until the left-hand corner reaches the existing horizontal crease.

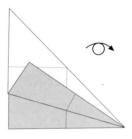

4. Turn over.

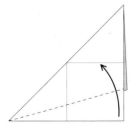

5. Fold the bottom edge upward, starting from the left-hand point, until the right-hand corner reaches the existing horizontal crease.

6. Fold the top half of the diagonal edge down to the existing horizontal crease, as shown.

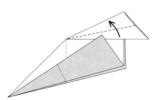

7. Fold the bottom edge of this flap back up to the outer edge.

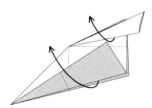

8. Unfold the previous two creases and open out along the diagonal fold.

A contemporary feel is achieved with the use of contrasting colors.

Note: You'll need two square pieces of paper; one for the blade and one for the handle.

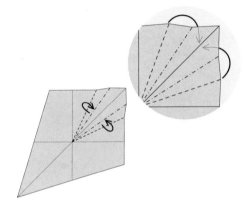

9. Reverse two of the creases so that they mirror each other, then bring the valley folds together under the central diagonal fold. The paper will no longer lie flat.

10. Mountain fold the very tip to remove the sharp point. Now that the blade is complete, let's fold the handle.

continued ▶

TO MAKE THE HANDLE

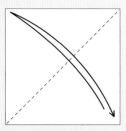

1. Start with a square with the white side up. Fold and unfold in half diagonally.

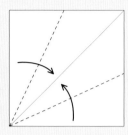

2. Fold the bottom and left-hand edges to the central diagonal crease.

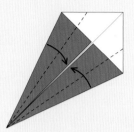

3. Fold both outer edges to the central diagonal crease again.

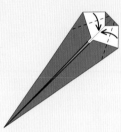

4. Fold the top point about one-third of the way down the white section, along the diagonal crease.

5. Fold both remaining raw edges to meet the central crease.

6. Turn over.

7. The handle is complete. Now to put the blade and handle together ...

TO ASSEMBLE THE TROWEL

Slightly open out the back of the handle and slip the two outer flaps around the diamond part of the blade (the part that's sticking up). This should keep the two parts together firmly.

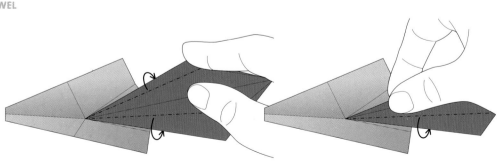

Practical pot

This useful container, designed by Colombian origami artist Leyla Torres, makes a sweet little plant pot for the origami garden. It would also be great for holding chocolates ... yum!

Skill level: 2

See page 52 for instructions for the square base.

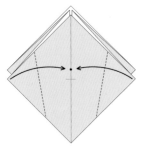

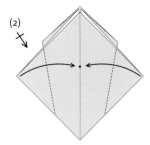

1. Start by folding a square base with the colored side facing out (see Steps 1–4, page 52). With the open edges facing upward, bring the tip of the top layer of paper down to meet the bottom edge and make a small pinch mark in the middle. Unfold.

2. Bring the left- and right-hand corners of the top layer of paper to meet on the central vertical crease, slightly above the pinch mark.

3. Turn over.

4. Repeat Step 2 on this side, using the folds behind as a guide.

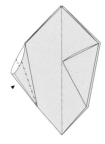

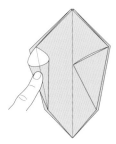

5. Unfold the left-hand side so that the flap is facing upward.

6. Insert your index finger into the top of this little flap and squash it down using the previous creases.

7. Flatten.

8. Mountain fold this section along the central crease so that the left-hand side ends up behind the right.

continued ▶

PROJECTS

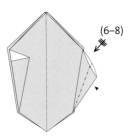

9. Repeat Steps 6–8 on the remaining three flaps.

10. Fold all the layers of the bottom point up to the base of the previous flaps. Crease well and unfold.

11. Fold the tip of the first layer of paper down as far as it will go and unfold.

12. Fold the tip down to the previous crease.

13. Bring the folded edge downward using the crease from Step 11.

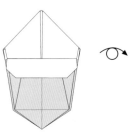

14. Turn over.

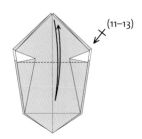

15. Repeat Steps 11–13 on this side.

16. Using the main central fold, bring the top large right-hand flap over to the left and the bottom left-hand flap over to the right.

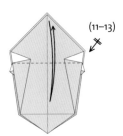

17. Repeat Steps 11–13 on both of these sides.

18. Push the left- and right-hand sides out. Pop out the base so that it opens into a square.

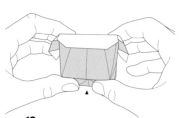

19. Use both hands to shape the pot.

Double-sided paper can really make these pots look special.

Skill level: 3

See page 52 for instructions for the square base.

Whether you are digging weeds, collecting apples from the tree, or having a picnic on the lawn, you'll need a basket in your garden. This traditional model will provide you with a very sweet container that's also perfect for holding candies.

Note: You will need two pieces of paper; a 4:4 square and a 1:4 rectangle.

TO MAKE THE HANDLE

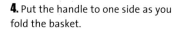

1. Start with a 1:4 rectangle with the white side up. Fold in half lengthwise and unfold.

2. Fold the top and bottom edges to the central crease, leaving a very small gap.

3. Bring the top edge down to the bottom edge, hiding the flaps.

4. Put the handle to one side as you fold the basket.

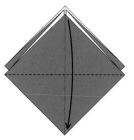

1. Start by folding a square base with the colored side facing out (see Steps 1–4 on page 52). With the open flaps facing upward, fold the tip of the top layer down to the bottom point.

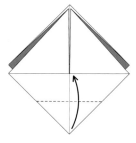

2. Fold the tip back up to the horizontal edge.

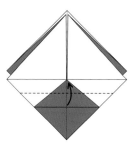

3. Fold the bottom edge of this flap up to the horizontal edge.

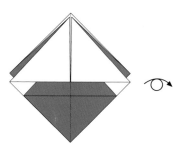

4. Turn over.

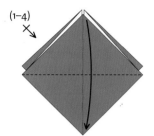

5. Repeat Steps 1–4 on this side.

6. Bring the top right-hand flap over to the left and the bottom left-hand flap over to the right.

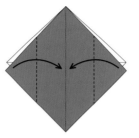

7. Fold the left- and right-hand corners to the center.

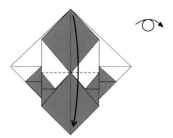

8. Fold the top point of the top layer all the way down to the bottom point. Turn over.

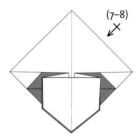

9. Repeat Steps 7–8 on the other side.

10. Unfold all creases back to the start of Step 3.

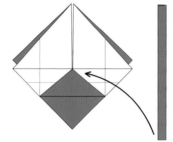

11. Locate the handle and insert it under the triangular flap.

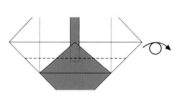

12. Fold the bottom edge, including the handle, back up along the existing fold. Turn over.

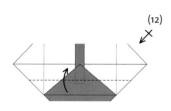

13. Repeat Step 12 on this side so that the handle is secured in place.

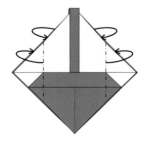

14. With the handle in place, refold the previous creases by first bringing the sides in then the tops down.

15. Fold all the layers of the bottom point up to the base of the handle. Crease well and unfold.

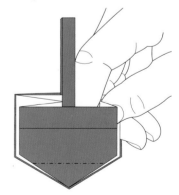

16. Insert your finger into the model and push out the base.

continued ▶

Thicker paper will make a stronger basket.

17. You can either leave your basket like this, or follow on to tidy away the two large flaps.

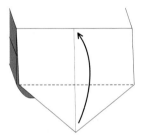

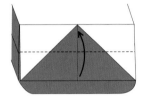

18. Fold the bottom point up to the middle of the top edge.

19. Fold the bottom edge up to the top edge.

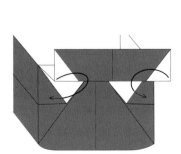

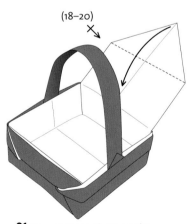

(18–20)

20. Lift this flap up and insert the bottom corners into the two small pockets underneath.

21. Repeat Steps 18–20 on the other flap.

Flower box

Designed by Tomoko Fuse, the Japanese queen of origami, this open box makes a beautiful table decoration. It may take a few attempts to collapse the first time, but you'll get there!

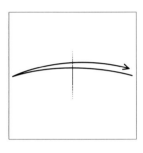

1. Start with a square with the white side up. Bring the right-hand edge over to the left-hand edge and make a small pinch in the middle of the paper. Unfold.

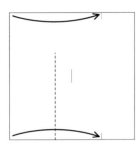

2. Bring the right-hand edge over to the central pinch mark. Make two more pinch marks at the top and bottom as shown. Unfold.

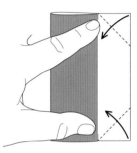

3. Align the top and bottom left-hand corners with the two pinch marks made in the previous step. Only flatten the bottom two-thirds of the paper as shown.

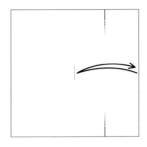

4. Hold the large flap down and fold the top and bottom right-hand corners over to meet the flap's raw edge.

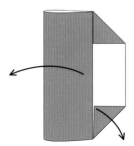

5. Unfold the large flap and the bottom right-hand corner.

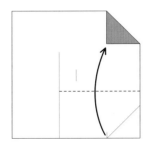

6. Fold the bottom raw edge up to the base of the top right-hand triangular flap. Crease only two-thirds of the way along the paper, as shown.

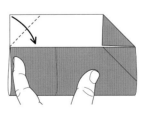

7. Keep the flap made in Step 6 pressed down and fold the top left-hand corner down to meet the flap's raw edge.

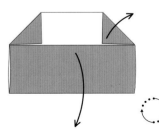

8. Unfold the bottom flap of paper and the top right-hand corner. Rotate the paper 90° clockwise.

continued ▶

These boxes make wonderful table decorations for a dinner party.

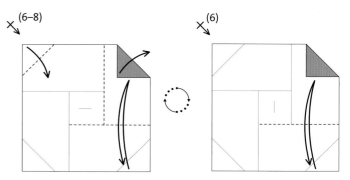

9. Repeat Steps 6–8 and rotate the paper 90° clockwise.

10. Repeat Step 6 and unfold.

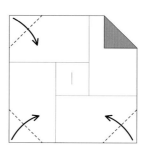

11. Fold the remaining three triangular flaps inward.

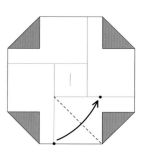

12. Bring the bottom raw edge up to meet the left-hand edge of the bottom right-hand triangular flap. Make a crease from the bottom point up to the first existing crease as shown.

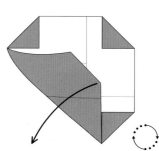

13. Unfold and rotate the paper 90° clockwise.

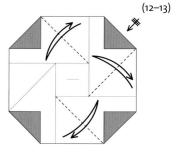

14. Repeat Steps 12–13 on the other three sides.

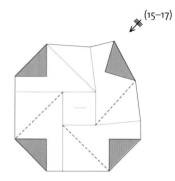

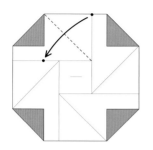

15. Fold the top raw edge down as shown, using the existing crease.

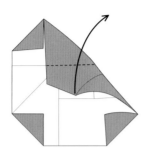

16. Fold this flap upward along the existing horizontal crease.

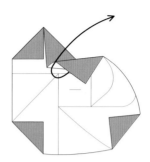

17. Unfold.

18. Repeat Steps 15–17 on the other three sides. This will reinforce the creases you'll need to collapse the box.

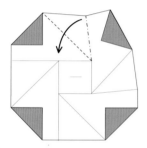

19. Start collapsing the paper by folding the top part down just like you did in Step 15.

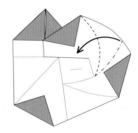

20. Place the paper in the palm of your hand and collapse the next section along the existing creases, as shown.

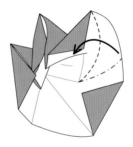

21. Continue to collapse the next section, as shown.

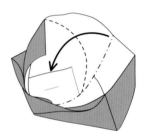

22. Collapse the last section in the same way. Use your thumb to push the paper all the way into the base of the box.

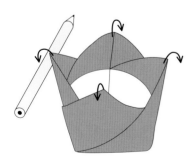

23. Curl the tips of the petals back if you wish.

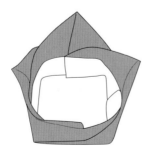

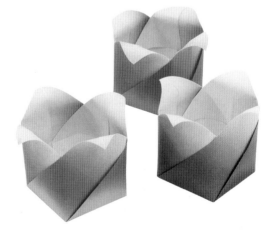

PROJECTS

Sitting dog

It's lovely to have a garden companion while pottering around outside. This fun and stylish dog was created by Eric Gjerde, an American origami artist.

Skill level: 1

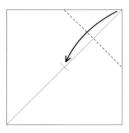

1. Start with a square with the white side up. Fold and unfold in half diagonally.

2. Bring the opposite points together and pinch at the center only. Unfold.

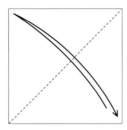

3. Fold the top right-hand corner to the pinch mark.

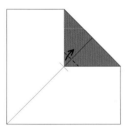

4. Fold the tip of the colored triangle about one-quarter of the way back.

5. Turn over.

6. Fold both edges to the diagonal crease.

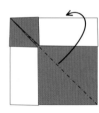

7. Mountain fold along the diagonal crease.

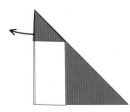

8. Pull out the flap of paper from inside the head.

9. Pinch the middle of the bottom colored edge.

10. Fold the bottom corner up from the pinch mark to form the tail. Unfold.

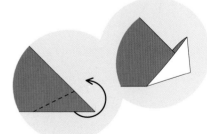

11. Use the existing creases to turn the tail inside out so the white side is now facing upward.

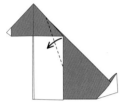

12. Fold the top flap from about halfway down the head to halfway down the white section.

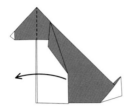

13. Fold the whole top flap over to the left.

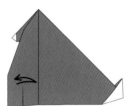

14. Bring the left-hand raw edge to the vertical crease and pinch the center of the bottom edge.

15. Fold the bottom left-hand corner to the pinch mark made in Step 14 and crease all the way up.

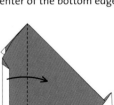

16. Fold the whole flap back to the right.

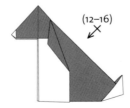

17. Repeat Steps 12–16 on the other side.

Using single-sided paper works really well to create extra definition.

Pet cat

Cats love to stroll around the garden, and are often very curious about the neighbors' patch too. This cat, designed by Ioana Stoian, is made using two squares of paper. You'll also need a marker pen to add character.

TO FOLD THE HEAD

Note: Make the head from a square of paper that is two-thirds the size of the square used for the body.

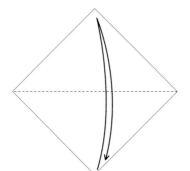

1. Start with a square with the white side up. Fold and unfold in half diagonally.

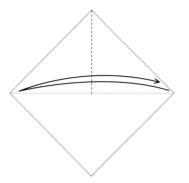

2. Bring the right-hand corner over to the left and crease the top half of the paper as shown. Unfold.

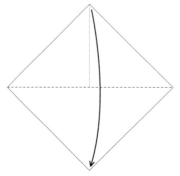

3. Fold the top corner back down to the bottom corner using the existing crease.

4. Fold the left- and right-hand points to the center of the top horizontal edge.

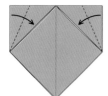

5. Fold the left- and right-hand vertical edges over as shown.

6. Unfold the top left- and right-hand flaps using the top diagonal edges as a hinge. Keep both flaps together (see Step 7).

7. Fold the top left- and right-hand points to the middle of the top horizontal edge using the existing creases.

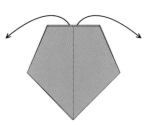

8. Completely unfold the left- and right-hand sections.

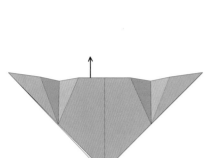

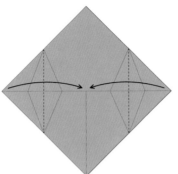

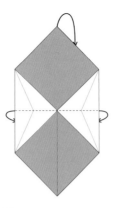

9. Unfold the paper so that the colored side is facing upward.

10. Fold the left- and right-hand corners to the center of the paper using the existing creases.

11. Push both vertical edges inward using the existing creases, and collapse the paper using the existing horizontal fold.

12. Bring the bottom point of the top layer of paper up to the middle of the top horizontal edge, and pinch the center. Unfold.

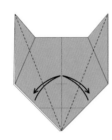

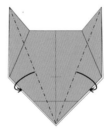

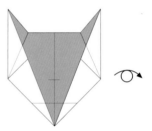

13. Fold the bottom corners of both layers of paper up to the pinch mark, and unfold.

14. Fold and unfold the bottom left- and right-hand raw edges of the top layer of paper over to the central vertical crease.

15. Mountain fold the top layer of paper along the creases made in the previous step.

16. Turn over.

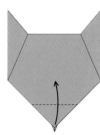

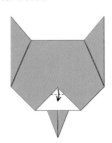

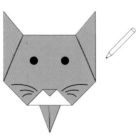

17. Fold the bottom corner of the top layer of paper upward along the existing crease.

18. Fold the very tip back down to form the nose.

19. If you like you can use a marker pen to give your cat some eyes and whiskers.

continued ▶

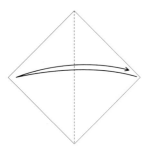
TO FOLD THE BODY AND JOIN IT WITH THE HEAD

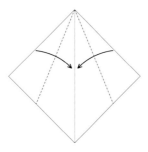

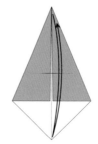

1. Start with the larger square with the white side up. Fold and unfold in half diagonally.

2. Fold the top left- and right-hand edges over to the central crease.

3. Bring the top point down to the bottom corner and make a small pinch mark in the center.

4. Fold the top point down to the previous pinch mark.

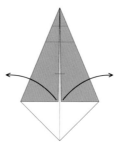

5. Fold the point back up to the center of the top horizontal edge.

6. Unfold the previous two steps.

7. Open up the left- and right-hand flaps.

8. Using the existing creases, bring the top point down to the pinch mark in the center of the paper.

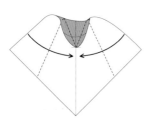

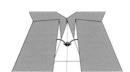

9. Fold the edges of the paper in toward the center along the existing diagonal creases.

10. Insert the back spike of the cat head into the pocket you have just made.

11. Open the left and right body flaps slightly to allow you to fold both points underneath—the head spike within the spike of body paper—upward along the existing crease.

12. Close the left and right body flaps back over to the central crease.

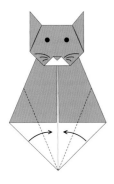

13. Fold the bottom left- and right-hand edges of the body up to the central vertical crease.

14. Turn the paper over.

15. Fold the bottom point up to the center of the top horizontal edge.

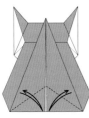

16. Fold the right-hand edge of the triangle down to the bottom edge, only creasing halfway, and unfold. Repeat on the left-hand side.

17. Using the creases from the previous step, bring the left- and right-hand edges of the triangle down to the bottom edge simultaneously. Fold the tail to the left or to the right to flatten the paper.

18. Turn over.

19. You can leave the tail behind or bring it around to the front by folding the very tip over to the front of the body.

Experiment with different colors and patterns to make unique kitties.

Friendly bunny

This adorable bunny, by Chinese creator Jacky Chan, will even carry something around for you. Using double-sided paper will give you color on the inside as well as the outside, but single-sided paper looks fun, too!

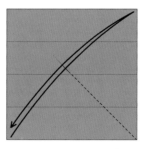

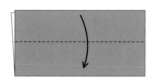

1. To create a bunny with colored ears and a white body, start with a square with the white side up. Fold the bottom edge up to the top edge.

2. Fold the top raw edge down to the bottom edge.

3. Turn over.

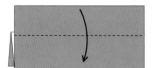

4. Fold the top edge down to the bottom edge.

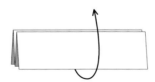

5. Unfold all steps so that the colored side is facing upward.

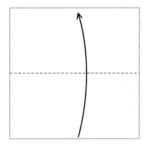

6. Bring the bottom left-hand corner over to the top right-hand corner. Only crease the bottom half of the diagonal as shown. Unfold.

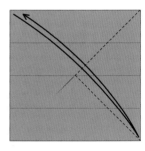

7. Bring the bottom right-hand corner over to the top left-hand corner. Only crease the top half of the diagonal as shown. Unfold.

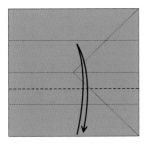

8. Fold and unfold the bottom raw edge up to the third horizontal crease.

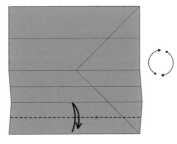

9. Fold the bottom raw edge up to the first horizontal crease. Unfold and rotate the paper 180°.

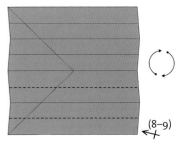

10. Repeat Steps 8–9 on the bottom half of the paper so that the square is divided into eight equal strips. Rotate the paper 180°.

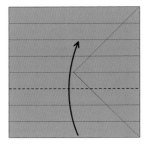

11. Fold the bottom raw edge up to the sixth horizontal crease.

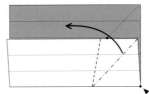

12. Pivot the bottom right-hand corner upward, using the existing creases, until it reaches the diagonal fold of the bottom layer of paper.

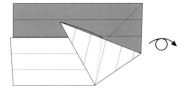

13. Flatten. Turn over.

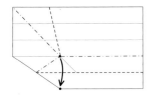

14. Bring the top dot down to the bottom dot using the existing creases, as shown. The left-hand side will not lie flat.

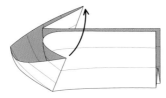

15. Flatten the left-hand side of the paper to match the paper behind it.

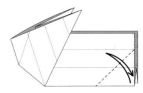

16. Fold and unfold both bottom right-hand corners up to the second existing horizontal crease, as shown.

continued ▶

17. Make a crease between the two dots, as shown. This will be very similar to the existing crease and will be used later on. Rotate the paper 90° counterclockwise.

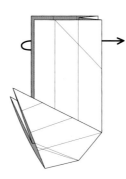

18. Bring the bottom layer over to the right-hand side, opening out the top part of the paper. The paper will look like a large arrow, as shown in Step 19.

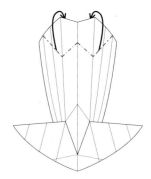

19. Make all of the creases that form a "W" at the top of the model into mountain folds. Push the top edge of the paper toward the inside of the model, as shown in Step 20.

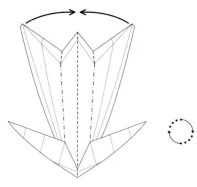

20. Bring both sides of the paper back together and rotate it 90° clockwise so that it is horizontal again.

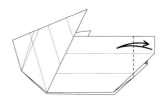

21. Fold the right-hand edge of the top layer of paper over toward the left so that it matches up with the inside edge behind it. Unfold.

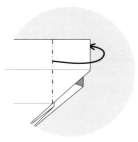

22. Fold the paper behind the top flap using the crease you have just made.

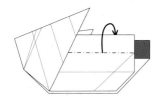

23. Fold the top layer of paper down along the top horizontal mountain fold. On the right-hand side the paper will land in the middle of the "W," creating a lock. The left-hand side will not lie flat until the next step.

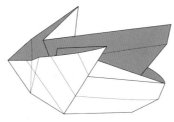

24. This is what the inside of the paper will look like at this stage.

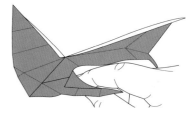

25. Follow the top folded edge with your index finger all the way to the left, as shown. Squash this triangular section down so that the existing crease line matches up with the folded edge.

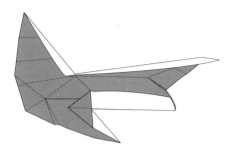

26. View of the inside.

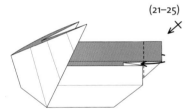

(21–25)

27. Repeat Steps 21–25 on the other side.

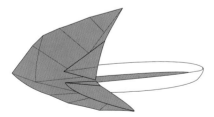

28. When both sides are completed the inside of your paper will look like this. Lay the paper back down and continue on to fold the ears.

continued ▶

Make a little fluffy tail with a cotton ball for an even cuter rabbit.

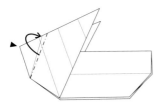

29. Push the left-hand point inward along the crease made in Step 17 so that it ends up between the ears.

30. Fold the top layer of paper down, making a crease between these two dots.

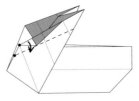

31. Fold this new edge downward as shown. The dot will land on the existing vertical crease and the right part of the paper will form an ear shape. It will not lie flat.

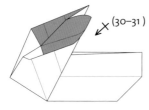

32. Repeat Steps 30–31 on the other ear.

33. Fold the paper at the base of each ear as shown. Repeat on the other side.

34. Fold the very tips of all four bottom corners toward the inside of the paper. This will round the body.

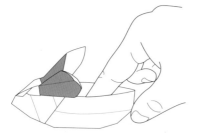

35. Insert your index finger into the middle section of the paper and press down.

36. Pop out the front part of the head as shown.

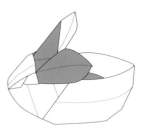

Acrobatic squirrel

Gymnasts of the garden, squirrels can be incredibly entertaining. Created by Ioana Stoian, this squirrel looks especially striking when made from paper that is the same color on both sides, although for clarity the instructions feature the usual white and colored origami paper.

Skill level: 3

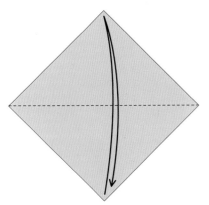

1. Start with a square with the colored side up. Fold and unfold in half diagonally. Turn over.

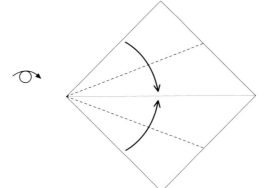

2. Fold the top and bottom left-hand edges to the central horizontal crease.

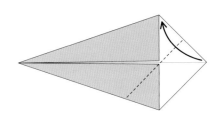

3. Fold the right-hand corner up to the top point. The bottom point will match up with the central crease.

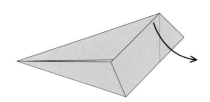

4. Unfold back to Step 3.

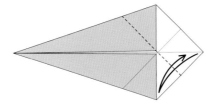

5. Repeat on the opposite side by folding and unfolding the right-hand corner to the bottom point.

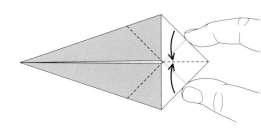

6. Using the creases you have just made, pinch together the top and bottom right-hand edges.

continued ▶

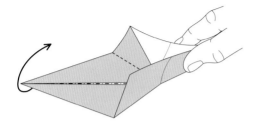

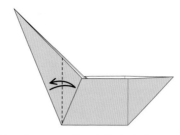

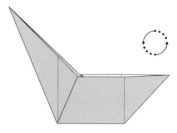

7. Keeping the right-hand side in your right hand, push up on the left-hand side so that the paper swings upward along the existing folds.

8. Flatten the paper, then fold the leftmost edges over as shown. Unfold.

9. Rotate the paper 90° counterclockwise and open out all the folds you have made so far.

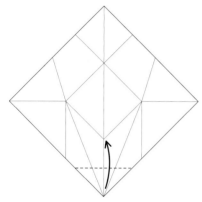

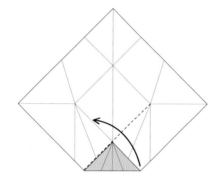

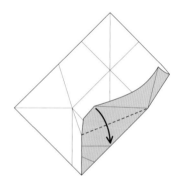

10. Check that your square is the right way up, then fold the bottom corner to the bottom point of the central diamond shape.

11. Fold the bottom right-hand edge over, using the bottom right-hand crease of the diamond, and continue the fold through the bottom part of the paper. The top right-hand part will not lie flat.

12. Use the existing diagonal crease as a hinge to bring the raw edge back down as shown. The paper will still not lie flat.

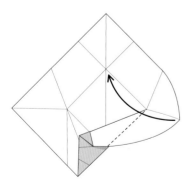

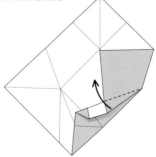

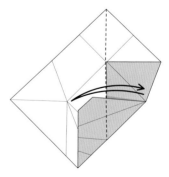

13. Bring the right-hand corner of the paper over to the top of the diamond shape. Now the paper will lie flat.

14. Fold the topmost bottom flap upward as shown.

15. Fold the right-hand side over to the left along the central vertical crease. Fold through all layers of paper. Unfold.

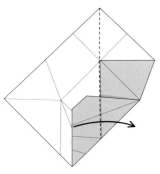

16. Bring the left-hand edge of the top layer of paper over to the right using the vertical crease made in Step 15.

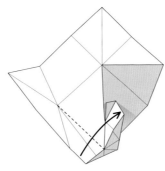

17. Fold the bottom left-hand raw edge of paper over to the right along the existing bottom left-hand crease of the central diamond shape. The paper will not lie flat.

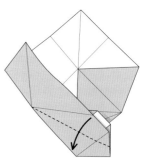

18. Use the existing diagonal crease as a hinge to bring the raw edge down as shown. The paper will still not lie flat.

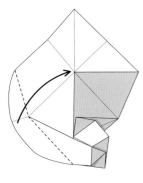

19. As before, bring the left-hand corner of the paper up to the top of the diamond shape.

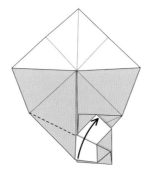

20. Fold the topmost bottom flap upward to mirror the flap behind it.

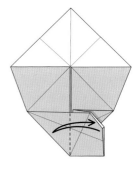

21. Fold the right-hand edges of the bottom flaps over to the left, creating a vertical crease that matches up with the existing one. Unfold.

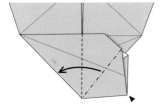

22. Push up on the bottom right-hand corner and, using the existing diagonal creases, squash down the paper as shown.

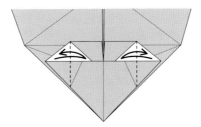

23. Now we will focus on the head. Fold and unfold the left- and right-hand points as shown.

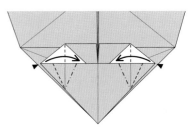

24. Open the bottom flap slightly and, using the existing creases, push the paper inward as shown. Flatten.

continued ▶

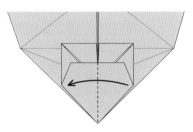

25. Fold the right-hand side of the face over to the left.

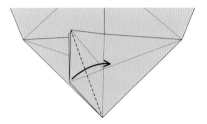

26. Fold as shown.

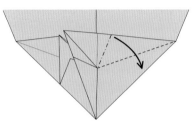

27. Bring the horizontal edge down to the bottom right-hand edge. At the same time, swivel the right-hand side of the head over to the right. Look at Step 28 to see how this should look.

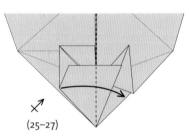

(25–27)

28. Repeat Steps 25–27 on the left-hand side of the head.

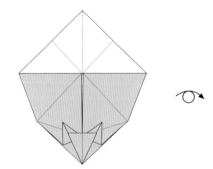

29. Turn the paper over.

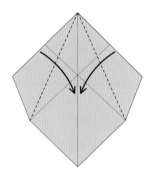

30. Fold the left- and right-hand raw edges along the central vertical crease.

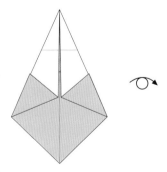

31. Turn over.

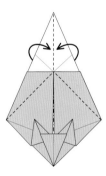

32. Use the existing creases to collapse the paper just as you did in Steps 6 and 7.

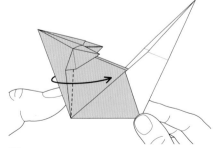

33. Hold the body together in one hand. Insert your thumb into the front slit and push all layers of the paper to the right.

Slightly dampening the edges will allow you to shape the paper to create soft curves for your squirrel.

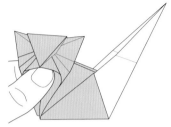

34. Use your thumb to flatten this front part of the paper all the way up to behind the eye sockets.

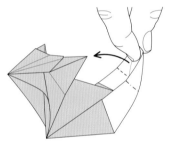

35. Shape the tail by bringing it down toward the head and then back slightly.

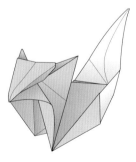

36. You may wish to fold the very tip of the nose downward and continue shaping the face until you are pleased with the final result.

Index

Credits

Quarto would like to thank the following origami artists for kindly contributing their designs for inclusion in this book:

Berty, Viviane, www.flickr.com/photos/vivianedespapiers, Jenny Wren, pages 79–81

Blanco, Ángel Écija, Busy Bee (with Leyla Torres), pages 46–49

Brown, Wayne, Night Owls, pages 82–84 and Perching Branch, page 85

Chan, Jacky, www.jackychan.org, Friendly Bunny, pages 116–120

Fuse, Tomoko, Flower Box, pages 107–109

Gjerde, Eric, www.ericgjerde.com, Slow Snail, pages 33–36 and Sitting Dog, pages 110–111

Klein, Isa, www.isaklein.com, Striking Butterfly, pages 44–45

Riesel, Alison, https://instagram.com/bloomeachday, Summer Dress, pages 90–91

Torres, Leyla, www.origamispirit.com, Busy Bee (with Ángel Écija Blanco), pages 46–49 and Practical Pot, pages 101–103

Author acknowledgments

I would like to thank Quarto for giving me the opportunity to make my second origami book. It has been a great pleasure being a part of their creative team for the last year.

My deepest gratitude goes out to all the origami artists and designers who have contributed their projects to this wonderful selection. Thank you!

A special thanks to Jane Rosemarin for letting me raid her collection of beautiful papers (on numerous occasions) and to Maria Sinaskaya for her attention to detail.

Lastly and most importantly, I would to thank my wonderful husband and biggest fan, Eric Gjerde. Your love, encouragement, and support are invaluable. I am incredibly lucky to have you by my side.